W9-AOV-838

Student Handbook for
AMERICAN GOVERNMENT

Student Handbook for
AMERICAN GOVERNMENT
Institutions and Policies / James Q. Wilson

Second Edition

Richard M. Pious
BARNARD COLLEGE

D.C. HEATH AND COMPANY
Lexington, Massachusetts   Toronto

TO THE STUDENT

This Handbook will help you to review and understand what you have read about American government in your textbook. The first part is a Study Guide that surveys the main points of each chapter and is intended to help you prepare for quizzes and examinations. The second part consists of exercises that deal with major topical areas of the text; they require you to do some research or examine data that support—or refute—the conclusions of political scientists. As you do these exercises, you will be turning to the sources of political scientists and using their skills. Your instructor may assign some of these to be done as special projects. Step-by-step directions have been given so that you can do these on your own.

For each chapter of the text, there is a corresponding chapter in the Handbook containing the following study aids.

Chapter Focus Read the Chapter Focus before reading the textbook chapter. It will help you to see the main points of the chapter. You may find it helpful to organize your notes around each objective, or to indicate next to each objective the pages in the textbook where that topic is discussed. After reading and reviewing the chapter, you should be able to fulfill all of the objectives.

Glossary Completion Supply the words that fit the definitions provided. You can find the answers to the exercise at the end of each Handbook chapter. Consult the glossary at the end of your textbook for other terms.

Common Misconceptions This is a list of some of the most common errors of fact or interpretation about American politics and government. If you have not read the text, you may make these errors on quizzes and examinations. Each chapter in the textbook contains arguments and evidence that refute these misconceptions. Indicate after each misconception the text pages where the topic is discussed.

Data Check   Your textbook contains many charts and tables that support the discussion. Each must be read carefully. This aid gives the purpose of the table, explains how the data are arranged, and relates the information to the argument of the chapter. (Only the most important charts and tables are highlighted in the Handbook.) You are then asked to write a paragraph that uses the data to support or refute a generalization about American politics or government.

State Your Case   Each chapter in the textbook explains important controversies about the nature and function of a political institution or process. This exercise asks you to express your personal values and perspectives on these issues. In the space provided in the Handbook, list the pros and cons for each side and summarize the evidence. Indicate the pages in the textbook where there is evidence that supports your position. Be prepared to argue your case in class.

Review Exercise   Use these questions to test yourself after you have read the chapter. Unlike multiple-choice questions, completions require you to *know* the answer, not merely to *recognize* it from alternatives. If you can answer half the questions correctly after reading the textbook chapter once, it is an indication that you are reading carefully. If you answer fewer than half correctly, you should consider that to be an indication that you may have trouble later on quizzes and examinations. (The answers are found at the end of each Handbook chapter.)

The textbook and Student Handbook have been prepared to assist you in becoming well informed about American government. In a democratic system it is the obligation of each person to participate and to acquire as much knowledge about politics and government as is possible. This course can, if you apply yourself, help you become an informed citizen.

CONTENTS

STUDY GUIDE

Part I The American System   **3**

    1. The Study of American Government *3*
    2. The Constitution *9*
    3. Federalism *15*
    4. American Political Culture *23*

Part II Opinions, Interests, and Organizations   **29**

    5. Public Opinion and Political Participation *29*
    6. Political Parties *37*
    7. Elections and Campaigns *45*
    8. Interest Groups *53*
    9. The Media *59*

Part III Institutions of Government   **65**

    10. Congress *65*
    11. The Presidency *73*
    12. The Bureaucracy *81*
    13. The Judiciary *87*

Part IV The Politics of Public Policy   **93**

    14. The Policy-Making Process *93*
    15. Business Regulation *97*
    16. Economic Policy *103*
    17. Social Welfare *109*
    18. Civil Liberties *115*
    19. Civil Rights *121*
    20. Foreign Policy *129*
    21. Military Spending *135*

Part V   The Nature of American Democracy   **141**

    22. Who Governs?   *141*
    23. To What Ends?   *143*

APPLICATIONS

Exercise 1.   The Constitutional Dimension   *147*
Exercise 2.   The Federal System   *155*
Exercise 3.   Surveying the Political Culture   *163*
Exercise 4.   Elections and Voting Participation   *167*
Exercise 5.   The Media   *175*
Exercise 6.   The Congressional Power Structure   *181*
Exercise 7.   Presidential Power   *189*
Exercise 8.   Implementing Judicial Decisions   *205*
Exercise 9.   The President, Congress, and Legislation   *219*
Exercise 10. The President, Congress, and Foreign Policy   *225*

STUDY GUIDE

PART I
The American System

1 The Study of American Government

CHAPTER FOCUS

After reading and reviewing the material in this chapter, you should be able to:

1. Identify the most important questions in the study of American government and politics.

2. Define the term "political power" and explain why officeholders do not have a monopoly on power.

3. Indicate which principles about power are legitimate to Americans. Contrast our ideas about power with those of other nations.

4. Describe several kinds of democracy, compare the pluralist and participatory approaches, and contrast both with democratic centralism.

5. Summarize the principles of Marxist, power elite, pluralist, and bureaucratic theories of political power.

GLOSSARY COMPLETION

1. .... The ability to influence who rules and to influence how rules make policy.

2. .... The legal or constitutional right to exercise power.

3. .... The acceptance of authority as proper, lawful, and just.

4. .... Rule by a political party committee over government in the name of the people.

5. .... The delegation of formal governmental authority to representatives elected by the people.

6. .... Theory suggesting that political power is exercised by a small group of people.

COMMON MISCONCEPTIONS

1. **"One can tell what policies an official will favor by knowing his or her race, religion, occupation, and other background characteristics."**
   False. President John F. Kennedy, a Roman Catholic, opposed aid to parochial schools, while President Lyndon B. Johnson, a Protestant, favored it. President Dwight D. Eisenhower, a former army general, cut back on the size of the army, while President Jimmy Carter, a former navy man who had served on a nuclear-powered ship, vetoed a bill because it contained funds for a nuclear aircraft carrier. Political alliances cannot be predicted by looking at social characteristics. In the 1960s white union leaders of the AFL-CIO were strong supporters of civil rights laws that were designed to aid blacks.

   Pages ....

2. **"The legitimacy of the American system rests solely on democratic values and practices."**
   False. Some nondemocratic values are important. These include the idea that government is limited and defined by a constitution and by laws, that minority rights sometimes take precedence over majority will, and that power must at times be checked and balanced and be decentralized through a federal system. Some officials, such as federal judges and Supreme Court justices, are not elected, nor are they expected to base their decisions on public opinion.

   Pages ....

3. **"Everyone agrees on the meaning of democracy."**
False. Communist nations claim they are democracies because one party governs in the name of the people. Third World nations often have one-party rule, but they say they govern in the name of the people. Western parliamentary regimes, some of them with hereditary monarchs as heads of state, also claim to be democracies. And the United States of America, where approximately half of the eligible voters do not vote in presidential elections, also claims to be a democracy.

Pages ....

4. **"Only government officials influence policy-making."**
False. Public opinion, interest groups, the investigative mass media, university researchers, all of these influence some policies. Sometimes demonstrations influence the government and lead to changes in policies. Consider the civil rights movement and the antiwar protesters.

Pages ....

STATE YOUR CASE

Some people think we should have more participatory democracy and also strengthen our system of representative government. They say we should elect all our public officials, ease voter registration requirements, and make sure that the will of the majority is reflected in all governmental decisions. Other people think that the important issues are so technical and complex that only well-informed citizens should be encouraged to vote, and that many policies should be left to the experts to handle, who by and large are appointed officials. What do you think? (In dealing with the pros and cons, you might consider your own experience as a student. Do you think participatory democracy would be beneficial in the running of your college? Or do you think that important decisions are appropriately made only by the faculty and the administration?)

REVIEW EXERCISE

1. An official with .... has a legal right to exercise power.

2. In the fifth century B.C. some citizens of a Greek .... could participate in making policy.

3. Joseph Schumpeter is identified with the theory of ....
...., and Max Weber is identified with the theory of ....

4. .... believe that the government is merely a reflection of underlying economic forces.

5. C. Wright Mills believed that government was dominated by a small group of individuals who formed a ....

6. The New England town meeting is an example of ....
....

7. The federal government of the United States of America was founded in the year ....

ANSWERS

Glossary Completion

1. political power
2. authority
3. legitimacy

4. democratic centralism
5. representative democracy
6. power elite

Review Exercise

1. authority
2. city-state
3. representative democracy;
   bureaucracy
4. Marxists
5. power elite
6. participatory or direct democracy
7. 1787

2 The Constitution

After reading and reviewing the material in this chapter, you should be able to:

1. Explain why the American colonists no longer considered the British constitution legitimate, and identify the "natural rights" they sought to protect through revolution.

2. List the political goals of the Revolution and indicate the basis for legitimacy of the American system.

3. Describe the problems the states had with the Articles of Confederation, and demonstrate why government under the Articles failed.

4. Show how differences among delegates to the Constitutional Convention were related to the experience of the states, and explain why most delegates favored limited government and representative rather than pure democracy.

5. Relate the principles of separation of powers and federalism to Madison's views about human nature in politics.

6. Explain why the Constitution could not be ratified without a commitment to a national bill of rights, and describe the rights guaranteed by the Bill of Rights.

7. Summarize Charles Beard's theories about the motives of the Framers and describe arguments used to refute them.

GLOSSARY COMPLETION

1. .... A set of principles, either written or unwritten, that constitutes the fundamental law of the state, and that establishes, defines, and limits the scope of political power and authority.

2. .... Rights ordained by God, discoverable in nature and history, and essential to human progress.

3. .... Rebellion of ex-Revolutionary War soldiers and officers in western Massachusetts.

4. .... A league, compact, or agreement among sovereign states to delegate powers to a central government.

5. .... The agreement at the national convention of 1787 that resolved the dispute over representation in the proposed House and Senate.

6. .... A system by which a national government exercises the sovereign power of the nation, while other powers are reserved to states, shared by states and the national government, or exercised solely by the national government.

7. .... Name given to those opposed to ratification of the Constitution in 1787–1788 (not to be confused with the political party organized by Jefferson and Madison under the same name in the 1790s).

8. .... Name given to the first ten amendments to the Constitution.

9. .... Name given to those favoring ratification of the Constitution (not to be confused with the political party organized by Hamilton in the 1790s).

COMMON MISCONCEPTIONS

1. **"The American Revolution pitted the poor against the rich."**
   False. The Revolution was not primarily a social or economic movement. Revolutionists included people from all social classes.

   Pages ....

2. **"Americans knew exactly the kind of government they wanted to establish after the Revolution."**
   False. For several years the states experimented with the Articles of Confederation, and they did not all agree that a new national government was needed. At the Convention the Framers disagreed as to the form a new government should take. The final version of the Constitution was the product of compromise, and it was considered an experiment by those who created it.

   Pages ....

3. **"The system of separation of powers was designed to produce the most efficient government possible."**
   False. It was designed to preclude tyranny and autocracy. The Framers were willing to sacrifice some efficiency in order to check and balance national institutions. (They did, however, expect the national government to be more efficient than the one discarded under the Articles of Confederation.)

   Pages ....

4. **"The Constitution did not deal with the question of slavery."**
   False. The Constitution provided that the slave trade could continue for twenty years, that fugitive slaves were to be returned to their masters, and that in apportioning representatives to the House, slaves (called "other persons") would count three-fifths as much as free persons in each state.

   Pages ....

5. **"The Constitutional Convention consisted of factions that voted against each other on the basis of different economic interests."**
   False. The economic interests of the Framers were diverse: some were debtors and some creditors, some merchants and some slave-holders. Divisions were not along obvious economic lines but reflected differences in political principles, regional interests, and state size.

   Pages ....

STATE YOUR CASE

Some people—following the Founders—believe that those who exercise power are likely to be corrupted and that the best government is one in which checks and balances can prevent the abuse of power. Other people believe that in a democracy rulers are ennobled through the exercise of power and that checks and balances get in the way of good and wise leaders who are trying to accommodate themselves to the will of the people as they provide the most effective government possible. Which theory of human nature do you think better explains the behavior of recent presidents and congressional leaders? Do you think—based on the events in your lifetime—that the checks and balances system has outlived its usefulness?

REVIEW EXERCISE

1. The Declaration of Independence contained 27 paragraphs of complaints against ....

2. After independence most states adopted written ....

3. The document of government for the national government between the Revolution and 1787 was known as the ....

4. Shays's Rebellion in the state of .... prevented the .... from sitting.

5. The Virginia Plan was favored by the .... states.

6. The two principles that formed the basis for the Constitution and that created the structure of government were .... and ....

7. The Constitution guarantees the right to a trial by .... in federal .... cases.

8. The structure of the Senate and House was set by the .... Compromise.

9. The first complete draft of the Constitution was prepared for the Convention by the Committee on ....

10. There can be no .... test or qualification for holding federal office.

ANSWERS

Glossary Completion

1. constitution
2. natural rights
3. Shays's Rebellion
4. confederation
5. Great Compromise
6. federalism
7. Antifederalists
8. Bill of Rights
9. Federalists

Review Exercise

1. the British monarch and his ministers
2. constitutions
3. Articles of Confederation
4. Massachusetts; courts
5. large
6. separation of powers; federalism
7. jury; criminal
8. Great
9. Detail
10. religious

3 Federalism

CHAPTER FOCUS

After reading and reviewing the material in this chapter, you should be able to:

1. Distinguish between a national system and a federal system of government, and contrast the decentralization of administrative functions in both systems. Then compare the British, French, and American methods of decentralizing political power.

2. Assess the intentions of the Founders and indicate why they believed a federal structure could limit powers and preserve liberties. What mechanisms did they believe would accomplish these ends? Contrast Hamilton's view of federalism with Jefferson's.

3. Describe the facts in the case of *McCulloch* v. *Maryland,* give the decision of the Court, indicate its reasoning, and assess the significance of the decision for the federal system. Describe the system of dual federalism and the problems of maintaining such a system.

4. Show why Congress and government officials are responsive to state and local constituencies in the passage and administration of national laws. Explain why the intergovernmental grant system is an example of such responsiveness. Explain why members of Congress like categorical grants and why state officials prefer block grants. Assess the effectiveness of the intergovernmental lobby.

5. Discuss the rivalry among the states, especially between the Sunbelt and Snowbelt. Explain the significance of the census in the federal system.

6. Explain why it is so difficult for the federal government to control intergovernmental programs (i.e., programs administered by state and local governments using federal funds), and indicate under what circumstances a federal agency has little power. Discuss the difference between "mandate" and "condition of aid." Explain why federalism leads to variations in public policy at the state level.

GLOSSARY COMPLETION

1. .... Regime in which states are sovereign and the national government is allowed to do only that which the states permit.

2. .... Regime in which sovereignty is shared, so that on some matters the national government is supreme and on others the states are supreme.

3. .... The belief that a state could refuse to enforce a federal law which in its opinion exceeded the constitutional powers of the federal government.

4. .... The belief that the federal government is supreme in its sphere, the states supreme in theirs, and the two spheres must remain separate.

5. .... A type of grant-in-aid for a specific purpose as defined by federal law.

6. .... Type of grant-in-aid that consolidates previously existing grants.

7. .... System for distributing federal funds to states and localities based on a formula, with almost no restrictions on local use.

8. .... The view that the powers of the national government should be limited, and that the chief

threat to liberties comes from the central government.

9. .... A law or court ruling directing states or cities to take certain actions.

10. .... A requirement attached to a grant from the federal government.

COMMON MISCONCEPTIONS

1. **"The Framers set forth a federal system that has endured with little change or controversy."**
   False. The system began with the tension between Hamiltonian and Jeffersonian ideas. Later there were problems over the doctrine of nullification. Eventually the Civil War settled issues involving the states' right to secede. In modern times there are disputes between liberals and conservatives over the scope of grant-in-aid programs. Throughout American history the federal system has been controversial, and almost every issue of domestic politics involves an aspect of federalism.

   Pages ....

2. **"The national government spends most of its money and enforces most of its laws directly on individuals."**
   False. It operates primarily through state and local governments by using the intergovernmental system. When the federal government expands its functions, this usually means that state and local governments expand theirs also.

   Pages ....

3. **"Liberal Democrats expand the intergovernmental grant system, and conservative Republicans always contract it."**
   False. Between 1970 and 1976, when Republicans were in the White House, federal aid to state and local governments went from approximately $24 billion to almost $60 billion. Prior to President Reagan, Republican presidents did not cut the system but presided over its expansion.

   Pages ....

4. **"Ever since the early 1970s, most federal aid has been distributed without federal controls through bloc grants and revenue sharing."**
   False. Categorical grants continued to grow faster than revenue sharing,

and controls were placed on bloc grants. However, between 1975 and 1978, revenue sharing increased by 11 percent, while categorical grants increased by 56 percent.

Pages ....

DATA CHECK

TABLE 3.1 Federal Aid to State and Local Governments, 1950–80, p. 56

1. Note that total federal aid in every five-year period since 1955 (except 1960–65) has almost doubled from the previous amount.

2. Note that between 1975–80 the total federal aid expressed in dollars almost doubled, while there was virtually *no* increase in this aid as a *percentage* of federal outlays or state and local outlays. Can you figure out why? (Hint: consult Table 2.1)

3. Use the data in this table to support or refute the following proposition: in cutting back massively on aid to states, Ronald Reagan is only doing what Republican Presidents Eisenhower, Nixon, and Ford have done.

FIGURE 3.1 Federal Grants to State and Local Governments, p. 55

1. The vertical axis indicates billions of dollars of grants to state and local governments. The horizontal axis indicates the fiscal years in which payments were made. The line labeled "Total" is the sum of five subtotals: highways, other human resources, employment and training, other grants, and general revenue sharing. To compute subtotal amounts, subtract the lower line from the higher. Thus, general revenue sharing is not $74 billion in FY 1977, but it is $74 billion minus $68 billion, or approximately $6 billion.

2. Note the sharp rise in many categories which began in 1974. These increases occurred primarily in other human resources, other grants, and employment and training.

3. Grants to state and local governments at the end of the Kennedy–Johnson

years, FY 1969, stood at approximately $20 billion, while at the end of the Nixon–Ford years, they totaled over $60 billion.

4. Use the data in this figure to support or refute the following proposition: As a result of Republican victories in 1968 and 1972, the federal grant system suffered a sharp slowdown in its rate of growth.

STATE YOUR CASE

Some people think that federalism allows states to block action, prevent progress, upset national plans, protect powerful local interests, and cater to the self-interests of hack politicians. Other people think that the federal system is a laboratory for experimentation and a vital element of diversity in the American system. Do you think that state governments should be abolished, weakened, left as they are, or strengthened?

REVIEW EXERCISE

1. In the years .... the United States experimented with a confederation form of government.

2. .... has the power to admit new states to the Union.

3. An existing state cannot be merged with all or part of another state without the consent of ....

4. The Constitution may not be amended to provide for unequal representation of states in the ....

5. If a treaty conflicts with state law, the .... is supreme over the ....

6. If a law of Congress conflicts with state law, the law passed by the .... is supreme.

7. Under Calhoun's doctrine of nullification a state would have the right to refuse to enforce laws of the ....

8. Under the doctrine of .... states are held to be supreme within their sphere of action.

9. Land-grant colleges were one of the first examples of a federal .... program.

10. In FY 1979 the federal government spent approximately $........................... billion in support of state and local governments.

11. General revenue sharing distributes about $.......................... billion.

12. President Reagan favors converting .... grants into .... grants.

13. By 1981 block grants accounted for .... percent of all federal grants to states and localities.

14. The power to "make all laws which shall be necessary and proper" to carry out the functions of Article I of the Constitution was granted to ....

ANSWERS

Glossary Completion

1. confederal
2. federal
3. nullification
4. dual federalism
5. categorical grant
6. block grant
7. revenue sharing
8. states' rights
9. mandate
10. condition of aid

Review Exercise

1. 1776–1787
2. Congress
3. that state
4. Senate
5. treaty; state law
6. Congress
7. federal government
8. dual federalism
9. grant-in-aid
10. $85
11. $6
12. categorical, block
13. 18
14. Congress

4 American Political Culture

CHAPTER FOCUS

After reading and reviewing the material in this chapter, you should be able to:

1. Define the term "political culture" and list its most widely shared values.

2. Compare the political culture of the United States with those of Great Britain, Germany, Italy, Mexico, Sweden, and Japan.

3. Trace the sources of the American political culture and indicate the significance of Puritan theology and the "congregational" model of church organization.

4. Offer reasons for the absence of a high degree of class consciousness among Americans.

5. Describe the changes in the levels of popular satisfaction with, and trust in, government since 1958, and offer some reasons why these changes have occurred. Compare the sense of efficacy among U.S. citizens with the sense of efficacy amongst Europeans.

GLOSSARY COMPLETION

1. .... A patterned set of ways of thinking about how politics and governing ought to be carried out.

2. .... An enduring belief that a way of behaving or a certain state of affairs is desirable.

3. .... Sense of confidence in the ability to influence who runs the government and what policies the government will pursue.

4. .... Belief that one has an obligation to participate in political or civic affairs.

COMMON MISCONCEPTIONS

1. **"The preservation of democratic institutions depends exclusively on the kind of constitution a nation adopts."**
   False. Some constitutions are a façade, concealing a despotic regime that pays no attention to its provisions. In a democratic nation the political culture must be supportive of the constitution and of democratic rule. Attitudes transmitted by the family, schools, churches, and political parties all help strengthen or weaken the "rules of the game" and the stability of democratic governments.

   Pages ....

2. **"The political culture can be used to predict exactly how people will behave."**
   False. The United States has a political culture that emphasizes civic obligations, but rates of voting are low and actual participation is lower than generally reported. Nevertheless, shifts in attitudes may forecast changes in behavior.

   Pages ....

3. **"The people's trust in government has decreased solely as a result of Watergate."**
   False. Various measures of distrust and cynicism show increases between 1958 and 1970, with subsequent and greater increases occurring between 1972 and 1976. These findings match a decrease in trust of nonpolitical institutions in the late 1960s. The problems of distrust and cynicism did not start or end with Watergate.

   Pages ....

4. **"Unemployed American workers always exhibit strong class consciousness."**

   False. During the Depression of the 1930s, employed and unemployed workers often exhibited class consciousness. But such periods in American history are rare. Surveys taken in the 1970s showed the great majority of the unemployed did not identify with other unemployed or think their interests as a class were in opposition to those of management.

   Pages ....

DATA CHECK

FIGURE 4.1   The Growth of Mistrust of Government, p. 82

1. The vertical axis, "Percentage of citizens who feel mistrustful," refers to the percentage of respondents who gave "mistrustful" answers to the five questions listed. The horizontal axis shows years.

2. Some measures have increased steadily since 1958, while others began to increase between 1964 and 1968. Since 1968 almost all cynicism measures have increased dramatically.

3. Use the data in this figure to support or refute the proposition that the reason Americans are so cynical about government is that Watergate has destroyed their faith in the system.

FIGURE 4.2   The Growth of a Sense of Political Ineffectiveness, p. 85

1. The vertical axis refers to the percentage of respondents who agreed with the three statements listed—the percentage who did not believe they were "efficacious." The horizontal axis indicates years.

2. Note the increase in people's sense of political ineffectiveness since 1960.

3. Use the data in this figure to support or refute the proposition that the conduct of President Ford restored the faith of the American people in government after the Watergate revelations of the Nixon presidency.

TABLE 4.7 Percentage of Americans Tolerating Certain Acts, by Level of Education, p. 87

1. This table indicates the relationship between tolerance for the acts listed at the left and formal years of schooling. Respondents are classified by levels of schooling, and the percentage tolerating the act within each educational level is given. Notice that the columns may not be added, either vertically or horizontally. Instead, percentages are to be compared, on a "more or less" basis, only horizontally.

2. For example, tolerance for demonstrations or petitions to legalize marijuana was least among grade school graduates (24% and 33%) and greatest among college graduates (64% and 73%).

3. Sweep your eyes across the columns, from left to right, to determine how an increase in education affects tolerance.

4. Use the data in this table to support or refute the proposition that "have-not" whites can unite with blacks in a coalition for social change.

STATE YOUR CASE

Some people believe that a high degree of conflict between individuals and between citizens and government officials is inconsistent with a stable form of government. Others believe that the exercise of the First Amendment freedoms of speech, assembly, and petition for redress of grievances is essential for a strong democratic system. Is there such a thing as "too much" free speech? (In considering your answer, you might wish to debate the question whether Nazis, who would overthrow the government and who have advocated genocide against various groups in American society, should have the right to advocate their point of view. Would you set any special limits on the First Amendment rights of groups that have stated as their aim the overthrow of the present form of government?)

REVIEW EXERCISE

1. The southern states in secession modeled their government after the Constitution of ....

2. According to the Almond and Verba study, the nation whose people had the strongest sense of civic duty and of competence was ....

3. The Swedish political culture is more .... than participatory.

4. The .... churches provided a set of beliefs and an organizational experience that had a strong impact on American political culture.

5. In 1976 about .... percent of all Americans thought that the federal government was too powerful.

6. In 1976 only a minority of Americans without a college education was willing to permit demonstrations in favor of .... marijuana.

7. Since the 1950s, public support for the exercise of political freedoms in America has been ....

ANSWERS

Glossary Completion

1. political culture
2. value
3. political efficacy
4. civic duty

Review Exercise

1. the United States
2. the United States
3. deferential
4. Protestant
5. 50%
6. legalizing
7. increasing

PART II

Opinions, Interests, and Organizations

5 Public Opinion and Political Participation

CHAPTER FOCUS

After reading and reviewing the material in this chapter, you should be able to:

1. List the sources of our political attitudes, and indicate which are the most important. Assess the influence of various religious traditions on political attitudes.

2. Explain why there is no single cleavage between liberals and conservatives, and why there are cross-cutting cleavages. Explain the significance of these facts. Assess the significance of race in explaining political attitudes.

3. Define "political ideology" and give reasons why most Americans do not think ideologically. Summarize the "liberal" positions on the economy, civil rights, and political conduct. Describe the major "policy packages" in the Democratic party and indicate which groups in the Democratic coalition can be identified with each package.

4. Identify which "elite groups" have become liberal, and compare their present attitudes with the past political preferences of these groups. Discuss the "New Class" theory as an explanation for changes in attitudes. Analyze why these changes are causing strain in the political party system.

5. Summarize data on the levels of political activity, and indicate which involve mass participation. Indicate which socioeconomic factors affect rates of participation.

6. Summarize the two different explanations offered about voting behavior.

7. Describe ways in which mass opinion can influence the policies of the government.

GLOSSARY COMPLETION

1. .... When differences in political opinion are based on many factors, not just one.

2. .... *political ideology* A coherent set of beliefs about who should rule and what policies rulers should pursue.

3. .... A group that has a disproportionate share of a resource.

4. .... When measures of a social class are no longer associated with political views that have traditionally been ascribed to a group or class.

5. .... High-status people with liberal views.

6. .... *SES* Measurements of income and level of education used to rank people.

COMMON MISCONCEPTIONS

1. **"The Founders intended that the government be run by the will of the majority."**
   False. The Constitution provided for popular election for only one-half of one of the branches of government—the House of Representatives. They expected that factions and interest groups would influence the government, and that these factions should be controlled. But they did not expect that mass public opinion, as we know it today, would have a major impact on government.

   Pages ....

2. **"Differences of opinion in the United States are clearly related to differences in class."**
   False. Poor blacks and poor whites disagree on racial issues; Protestants and Jews of similar status often disagree on social welfare policies; and a majority of poor whites vote Republican, while a majority of poor blacks vote Democratic. Combinations of factors, including race, religion, region, and party identification, as well as status and occupation, determine political opinions.

   Pages ....

3. **"Most Americans take consistently liberal or conservative positions on issues."**

   False. Most Americans do not display ideological thinking. They may take liberal positions on some issues and conservative positions on others. They may be inconsistent—by supporting government social welfare programs, but at the same time applauding efforts to reduce government spending in general. There seem to be various combinations involving some liberal and some conservative positions, and each of these combinations attracts candidates and voters.

   Pages ....

4. **"Affluent people are always politically conservative."**

   False. The "New Class" of affluent, under-forty persons with technical, scientific, and professional occupations is often more liberal than business elites. "New Class" Democrats are likely to be more liberal than working-class Democrats.

   Pages ....

DATA CHECK

TABLE 5.2 Religion and Political Opinions, p. 94

1. The survey data were compiled for the 1976 election and do not reflect changes since then. This is a *bivariate* table (involving two quantities that can vary), and it attempts to show how in a particular election religious affiliation could be associated with political opinions.

2. Such a table does not imply causal relations. There is no reason to assume that one's religion causes one to have certain political beliefs, or that one's political beliefs cause one to choose a particular religion.

3. Only northern whites were surveyed. This would include most Jews and a large majority of Roman Catholics, but it would exclude most black Protestants (whose attitudes are liberal) and southern white Protestants (whose attitudes are moderate or conservative).

4. Use the data in this table to refute or support the argument that the major cleavage in American politics today is based on religious differences.

FIGURE 5.1   The Upper Middle Class Abandons the G.O.P., p. 113

1. The graph on the left shows changes in partisan self-identification between 1940 and 1976. The + figures 0 to 40 represent percentage differences in favor of the Republicans, while the − figures represent percentage differences in favor of the Democrats. An ascending line favors Republicans; a declining line favors Democrats.

2. A measurement of 0 means an even split between the parties, a measurement of + or −10 means a difference between the parties of 45% to 55%, a measurement of 20 means a difference between the parties of 60% to 40%, and so on.

3. Until the 1960–1964 period, the Republicans had a favorable margin among all three groups; but between 1964 and 1976 the trend has moved in favor of the Democrats, and they have won favorable margins.

4. The graph on the right uses the same margin measurements to determine changes in the congressional vote between 1940 and 1976. Note the same trends, and the same crucial period, 1960–1964, when Democrats gained the margin over Republicans. Also note that the margins in congressional voting were greater for Republicans in the earlier period and greater for the Democrats in the later period than the margin of party identification shown in the graph on the left.

5. Use the data in these graphs to support or refute the argument that young people can be counted on to vote Democratic, and that college-educated and business executives can be counted on to vote Republican.

TABLE 5.8   Attitudes of "New Class" and "Old Class" Democrats on Social and Cultural Issues, p. 115

1. The percentages in each column refer to those in each class who agree with the question. If 59% of the "New Class" Democrats agree with the statement that divorce should be easier to obtain, then 41% of such Democrats will disagree with that statement.

2. The purpose of the table is to show that certain age, education, and occupation characteristics may be associated with attitudes on social and cultural issues. Data are from national surveys conducted between 1972 and 1977. Respondents were categorized by "class."

3. One can infer that belonging to a different class may "cause" a difference in attitude, but such an inference is not directly proved by the data. The data do make it it clear that class characteristics are *associated* with differences in attitudes.

4. Remember, not *all* "Old Class" or "New Class" members agree with others of their "class." Even though 59% of the "New Class" Democrats want divorces to be made easier, a substantial 41% want divorces to remain hard to get. Even though 55% of "Old Class" Democrats want tougher laws on pornography, 45% of that group disagreed with that position.

5. Use the data in the table to support or refute the argument that Democratic party identifiers agree with the historic identification of their party with the civil rights struggles of blacks.

STATE YOUR CASE

Some people think that voters are rational, issue oriented, and capable of making informed choices about public policy. Others believe that most voters choose on the basis of party identification, parental socialization, and other environmental factors. Still others believe that in the age of mass media and "Madison Avenue" selling techniques, most people will vote for the candidate with the slickest advertising campaign. How do you think most people vote? (In considering your answer, you might wish to recall your own behavior as a voter. Or you might want to examine political commercials in an election year. On what basis do they appeal to voters?)

REVIEW EXERCISE

1. Most high school seniors share the party identification of their
   ....

2. By religion, families that are most liberal are ....

3. In terms of ideology, a college education makes students more
   ....

4. Nonmanual workers in the United States are shifting away from the
   .... party.

5. By the 1970s blacks had become overwhelmingly .... in terms
   of ideology.

6. In terms of ideology, members of the "New Class" are likely to be
   ....

7. About .... percent of the population can be classified as political
   inactives.

8. Among persons of the same socioeconomic status, blacks tend to participate
   at a .... rate than whites.

9. An example of a policy that was strongly influenced by public opinion would
   be ....

10. An example of a policy not strongly influenced by public opinion would be
    ....

ANSWERS

Glossary Completion

1. cross-cutting cleavages
2. ideology
3. elite
4. class inversion
5. new class
6. socioeconomic status

Review Exercise

1. parents
2. Jewish
3. liberal
4. Republican
5. liberal
6. liberal

7. 22%
8. higher
9. social security; Medicare; unemployment compensation
10. school busing; Electoral College reform; the foreign aid program

6 Political Parties

CHAPTER FOCUS

After reading and reviewing the material in this chapter, you should be able to:

1. Define the term "political party" and contrast the structure of the European and American parties, paying particular attention to the federal structure of the American system and the concept of party identification.

2. Trace the development of the party system through its four periods and offer reasons why parties have been in decline since the New Deal period.

3. Describe the structure of a major party and distinguish powerful from powerless party organs. Discuss the difference between "representational" and "organizational" party structure, and indicate why the Democrats use one system and the Republicans use another.

4. Define intraparty democracy and indicate its effect on the Democratic nominating conventions in the last few contests. Evaluate the relative strengths of state party bosses in recent years, and discuss the increasing importance of primaries in relation to the "boss" system at conventions.

5. Describe the machine, discuss its functions, and trace its decline. Contrast its structure with that of ideological and reform parties.

6. Offer two explanations for the persistence of the two-party system. Explain why minor parties form and discuss different kinds of parties. Analyze the reasons why they are so rarely successful.

7. Describe some of the issue differences between delegates at Democratic and Republican conventions, and indicate if there are major differences between the parties.

GLOSSARY COMPLETION

1. .... *party* .... Group that seeks to elect candidates to office by providing them with a label by which they are known to the electorate.

2. .... *Congressional Caucus* .... Nominating system in which members of Congress chose a party's presidential nominee.

3. .... *direct Primary* .... System in which rank-and-file party members vote for the party nominee.

4. .... *national convention* .... System in which delegates elected by party members choose a presidential nominee.

5. .... *midterm Convention* .... Meeting at which party members discuss issues and modify party rules for selecting a president.

6. .... System whereby majority sentiment determines policies, candidates, and rules of a party.

7. .... *machine* .... An organization that rewards followers with tangible incentives such as patronage.

8. .... A group split off from a major party because of a dispute over candidate and platform.

COMMON MISCONCEPTIONS

1. **"National party organizations control state and local parties."**
   False. State and local parties control their own finances, membership, nominations for public office, and party platforms.

   Pages ....

2. **"The Founders believed a party system was essential for democracy."**
   False. They were suspicious of parties, viewing them as illegitimate factions. Neither the Federalist nor the Antifederalist party viewed political opposition as legitimate. Not until the 1830s and the rise of the Democratic

and Whig parties was party competition for office routinized and legitimated as part of the American system.

Pages ....

3. **"The American party system is highly ideological and issue oriented."**
False. The minor parties are the most ideological, which may account for their poor performance. The constituent units of the major parties, the state and local parties, were originally machines, and are now a mixture of machine, reform, or candidate-centered elements. They embrace a wide variety of social, economic, racial, and religious groups, which makes ideological appeals difficult. Instead, the major parties emphasize benefits for members of the voting coalitions, party identification, and the personalities of their candidates.

Pages ....

4. **"Major parties generally adopt proposals first made by minor parties."**
False. Ideological proposals of the left and right have generally not been adopted. Southern regional parties since the 1940s have not strongly influenced the Democratic party on most matters. Often a major party adopts something due to public opinion, which a minor party had previously proposed, but the relationship is usually coincidental rather than causal.

Pages ....

5. **"The delegates to national party conventions have accurately reflected the sentiments of rank-and-file members since the intraparty reforms of convention rules in 1972."**
False. Those who are likely to be chosen convention delegates, party activists, are more ideological or issue oriented than are the rank and file. Democratic delegates are more liberal, and Republican delegates more conservative, than party members. Paradoxically, the rule changes give activists more opportunity to make the party less representative of the sentiments of the rank and file.

Pages ....

6. **"There isn't a dime's worth of difference between the two major parties."**
False. When party rank and file are compared on issues, clear differences between the two parties emerge on economic, social welfare, and other issues. Members of Congress and delegates to national conventions also differ significantly along party lines.

Pages ....

DATA CHECK

TABLE 6.1 How Delegates to the Democratic and Republican Conventions Differ, p. 139

1. For each characteristic, the two sets of percentages indicate the proportion of convention delegates in each party with the characteristic. The numbers add up to more than 100 percent, since delegates each have many such characteristics (for example, woman, Roman Catholic, college educated, lawyer).

2. Which party seems to have greater social and religious diversity among its delegates? Which seems to have greater ideological diversity?

3. Does either party seem to represent women, blacks, young people, Catholics, or Jews way out of proportion to their percentage of the general population?

4. Note that a far greater percentage of elected Republican politicians attend conventions than do Democratic elected politicians. How do the party rules account for these differences?

5. How would you use the data in this table if someone told you that minorities were taking over the two-party system?

TABLE 6.3 How Party Delegates and Party Voters Differ, p. 153

1. Note the difference in ideological self-description between Democratic delegates and party members. Which group is more liberal?

2. Support or refute the argument that the reforms instituted by the Democratic party between 1968 and 1972 have made it more democratic and responsive to majority sentiment.

3. Which party has a closer fit between delegate and member ideology—Republican or Democratic? Which convention had a closer fit with the self-description of a sample of adult Americans?

TABLE 6.4 Policy Preferences of Voters Who Identify with Democratic and Republican Parties, 1980, p. 155

1. For each issue there are two positions, one liberal and one conservative. In each case the Democratic identifiers are more liberal than are the Republicans.

2. You should note which issues demonstrate differences of 10% or more between the parties.

3. Support or refute the argument that most Democratic voters oppose most Republican voters on the "social issues."

TABLE 6.5 Policy Preferences of Delegates to Democratic and Republican Presidential Nominating Conventions, 1972, p. 156

1. For each issue there are two positions, one liberal and one conservative. In each case the Democratic delegates are more liberal than are the Republicans.

2. Compare the positions of Republican voters in Table 6.3 and Republican delegates. Find the differences for each issue, and then compute the mean difference on all issues. Then do the same thing for Democratic voters and delegates. Which set of delegates seems to be more representative of rank-and-file voter sentiment?

3. Use the data in this table to support or refute the argument that the reforms instituted by the Democratic party between 1968 and 1972 have made its machinery more representative than that of its opponents.

STATE YOUR CASE

Some people think that the president should control the party structure at the national, state, and local levels and that he should also be the party leader in Congress. If a president had such control, the argument goes, it would enable him to run the government smoothly and efficiently. Others think that there should be more participation in party matters by rank-and-file voters, more intraparty democracy, and more autonomy for local party organizations, even if it might make things more difficult for leaders at the top of the government. Which do you think is more beneficial: greater presidential control over his party, or more intraparty democracy?

REVIEW EXERCISE

1. The oldest political parties in the world still in existence are found in
   ....

2. Instead of being chosen by party leaders, candidates for public office in the
   United States are generally chosen in ....

3. The followers of Jefferson in the 1790s called themselves ....
   ...., and the followers of Hamilton called themselves
   ....

4. The convention system begun in the 1830s replaced the ....
   .... as a means of nominating presidential candidates.

5. The Mugwumps were a faction of the .... party.

6. Progressives favored civil service reform to eliminate .... in government employment.

7. The ultimate source of authority over the party is the ....

8. Democratic party reformers in the 1970s sought to create a .... party.

9. Tammany Hall is an example of a .... organization.

10. The Hatch Act regulated the political activities of ....

11. The Socialist party is an example of a(n) .... party.

12. The Democratic party of Detroit is an example of a .... party.

13. The South is affiliated primarily with the .... party.

14. The only minor party that won the presidency was the .... party.

ANSWERS

Glossary Completion

1. party	5. midterm convention
2. caucus system	6. intraparty democracy
3. direct primary	7. machine
4. national convention	8. factional party

Review Exercise

1. the United States	8. representational
2. primaries	9. machine
3. Republicans; Federalists	10. federal civil servants
4. congressional caucus	11. ideological or minor
5. Republican	12. sponsored
6. patronage	13. Democratic
7. national convention	14. Republican

7 Elections and Campaigns

After reading and reviewing the material in this chapter, you should be able to:

1. Compare voter participation in the United States with turnout levels in Western European parliamentary democracies.

2. Describe the changes in election laws and practices that had the effect of increasing legal suffrage in the United States, and discuss the attempt in the late nineteenth century to decrease black voter participation. Explain the impact of the Voting Rights Act of 1965 and the Twenty-Sixth Amendment.

3. Summarize the theories used to explain the apparent decline of voter turnout in the 1890s, and assess the impact of registration and the use of the Australian ballot on turnouts. Discuss reasons for the decline in turnout since 1960.

4. Contrast the personalistic campaign organization with the party machine. Explain how primaries have weakened party organizations and contributed to the development of new campaign styles. Describe the problems a presidential nominee may encounter as a result of the positions he has staked out in the primaries. Summarize the impact of television on campaigning, especially at the precinct level.

5. Define realigning period and trace the occurrences of these periods in the past. Explain why critical elections lead to realignments and the significance of these elections for the party system.

6. List the various groups in the Republican and Democratic voter coalitions,

and contrast the composition of the two parties. Assess the impact of "single issue" groups on the party coalitions.

7. Contrast the pre- and post-1974 systems of campaign finance. Discuss the impact of television, primaries, and personalistic campaign organizations on the system of campaign finance. Explain how important money is in winning elections, and the motives of incumbents in supporting spending limitations.

GLOSSARY COMPLETION

1. *Straight ticket* .... Voting for all members of the same party.

2. *split ticket* .... Voting for members of different parties.

3. *poll tax* .... A tax paid to exercise the right to vote.

4. *primary* .... Election to choose a party nominee.

5. .... Election to choose officeholders.

6. *closed primary* .... Party contest open only to registered party voters.

7. *open primary* .... Party contest open to any registered voter.

8. *sound bite* .... Brief filmed or taped episode on news broadcast showing a candidate doing something.

9. .... A reorganization of coalitions so that one party gains dominance over another.

10. *PAC* .... Interest group set up by corporations, or unions to contribute to federal election campaigns.

COMMON MISCONCEPTIONS

1. **"There has been an increase in voter turnout in elections throughout American history."**
   False. Most legal barriers have been swept away, but this merely expands the *right* to vote. The actual turnout of voters (expressed as a percentage of

persons of voting age)—those who actually vote in elections—has apparently varied. It rose through much of the nineteenth century, declined sharply in the early twentieth century (some of this change may have been the result of ballot reforms), rose during the Great Depression, stabilized until the late 1960s, and is now undergoing a decline. The American turnout rate is now significantly lower than that of most other Western democratic systems.

Pages ....

2. **"Throughout the twentieth century blacks have been able to exercise the right to vote with little difficulty."**
   False.   Most legal restrictions against blacks were not instituted until the 1890–1910 period. Courts left many of these barriers standing, especially literacy tests. Not until the passage of the Voting Rights Act of 1965 did blacks vote in great numbers so that they became a mass electorate in the South.

   Pages ....

3. **"Because the United States holds more elections for more offices than most other nations, its party system is stronger than in most other nations."**
   False.   The American party system is weak. One party usually dominates all others in each state or locality, and highly competitive elections between the parties are uncommon in many states. Party structure continues to disintegrate. Campaigns once run by regular party organizations are now largely run by personal followers of candidates. The primary system weakens the strength of party organizations and also weakens party discipline. At the rank-and-file level there has been a weakening of strong partisanship and of strong party identification.

   Pages ....

4. **"Voters generally choose on the basis of issues presented during campaigns."**
   False.   As many as two-thirds of the electorate choose on the basis of party loyalty or personality themes rather than—or in addition to—issues. Many voters know how they intend to vote prior to the election campaign.

   Pages ....

5. **"Democrats usually win presidential elections because their coalition includes the young, the college-educated, the poor, and independents."**
   False.   More often than not, majorities of these groups vote for Republican presidential candidates. Consider the election of 1980.

   Pages ....

6. **"The reason for high rates of nonvoting is that there are cumbersome voter registration procedures in the states."**

   False. In states that have instituted registration by mail, registration on election day—or none at all—turnouts have not increased markedly. In some cases turnouts after these reforms were instituted actually declined. There is no clear evidence that a dramatic rise in turnouts would occur if registration procedures were eased in most states.

   Pages ....

DATA CHECK

TABLE 7.2   Policy Preferences of Voters Supporting George McGovern and Richard Nixon in 1972 Election, p. 171

1. The data were compiled for the 1972 presidential election, one in which the candidates tried to present different positions on a variety of issues. On the left is a list of five issues, offering a liberal-conservative dimension. The first two vertical columns show the difference between McGovern primary supporters and all Democratic voters. The last column provides attitudes of Democrats who voted for Nixon in the general election.

2. McGovern supporters in primaries were more liberal than other Democrats. Democrats who defected to Nixon were predominantly right of center.

3. On several issues, such as busing and decriminalizing the use of marijuana, a substantial minority or even a majority of McGovern supporters took the conservative position. But there is no issue on which Nixon supporters were predominantly liberal.

4. On some issues McGovern's primary supporters split into two camps of equal strength: these included amnesty and decriminalizing marijuana.

5. Use the data in this table to support or refute the proposition that in 1972 the candidates attracted voters solely on the basis of personality appeals and party identification.

TABLE 7.3   Percentage of Popular Vote by Groups in Presidential Elections, 1952–1980, p. 177

1. This table indicates how each set of identifiers (Republicans, Democrats, Independents) claims to have voted in a presidential election. For each year

the total percentages for each party equal 100%, divided among the various candidates. Columns are read down, to see how group support has changed from one election to the next. Columns are read across, to see how a candidate won his votes, whether he built a partisan or bipartisan coalition, and whether he won the independent vote.

2. Remember that these figures are based on what people said they did, not on actual voting results. Not everyone can remember what he or she did; not everyone wishes to report accurately. In surveys of this kind there is usually significant overreporting of voting, and also a bias toward the winner of the election.

3. With the exception of the 1964 election, Republican identifiers always gave over 80% of their support to the Republican candidate. Note that, except for 1956 and 1964, Democrats did not give as much as 85% of their vote to the Democratic candidate. How can you explain the fact that in a number of these elections the Democrat won?

4. Consider the extreme volatility of the independent voter. Between 1956 and 1960 Democrats raised their support among independents by 13%, between 1960 and 1964 by another 13%, and then in 1968 their margin decreased by 25%.

5. Use the data in this table to support or refute the argument that to win the White House a candidate must win the independent vote.

FIGURE 7.4 Trends in Split-Ticket Voting for President and Congressmen, 1920–1980, p. 185

1. The horizontal axis represents House congressional elections held in presidential election years. The vertical axis represents the percentage of "split-ticket" results: those House districts carried by a presidential candidate for one party and won by a congressional candidate of another party. Thus, a 10% figure would indicate that there were forty-three House seats involving "split-ticket" results.

2. Note the great jump in 1928. This was due to southern defections from the presidential ticket of the Democrats, because of the nomination of Roman Catholic Al Smith. If not for that unusual defection, the trend from 1920 to 1972 would be much smoother. Note the decline in 1976. How would you explain this? How would you explain the results in 1980?

3. How would you use the data in this table if someone told you that increasingly the performance of the party's presidential nominee in the campaign affects the prospects of the party's gaining or losing seats in Congress?

TABLE 7.4 Who Likes the Democrats?, p. 188

1. Percentages refer to the proportion of the group stating they voted for the Democratic presidential nominee in the indicated year.

2. Note which percentages are relatively stable (blacks, Catholics, Jews) and which swing from support of one party to support of the other (under 30, Southerners). Which groups have been predominantly Democratic? Republican?

3. Contrast the 1964 and 1972 results. Explain why in both cases the results seem so out of line with other elections.

4. Use the data in this chart to support or refute the argument that the Democrats were the party of blue-collar workers, Southerners, and the young.

5. In both 1968 and 1980 there were three major candidates. See if you can spot the crucial change in voting behavior of two groups, each of which "defected" from the Democrats in 1980.

TABLE 7.5 The Contribution Made to Democratic Vote Totals by Various Groups, 1952–1980, p. 189

1. Note the differences in percentages in this table compared to the group voting table. This table indicates the composition of Democratic vote totals. Thus, the percentage 41 listed in 1952 for Catholics means that 41% of the

Democratic vote that year came from Catholics, and does *not* mean that 41% of all Catholics in 1952 voted Democratic. (Note that the data in Table 7.4 indicated that in 1952, 56% of all Catholics voted Democratic.)

2. You can follow the trend by moving your eyes from left to right: the poor, Catholics, and central cities today account for less of the Democratic vote than they did previously, while blacks and the South are more important to the Democratic party coalition. Do you think the contribution of blacks to the coalition increased or decreased in 1980? Is an increase necessarily good for black Democrats? Why not?

STATE YOUR CASE

Some people think that elections are meaningless exercises in media manipulation, and that election results have no effect on the way the country is governed. Others argue that elections matter very much, and that differences between the parties and candidates are very real. What do you think? (It may be helpful for you to review what you have learned about parliamentary systems and responsible party government.)

REVIEW EXERCISE

1. There are approximately .... elective offices in the United States.

2. In the 1980 presidential election the turnout of the eligible population was approximately .... percent.

3. The Nineteenth Amendment to the Constitution greatly expanded the suffrage of ....

4. The .... Amendment to the Constitution lowered the voting age to eighteen.

5. Generally, the party with more voter defections in presidential elections will be the .... party.

6. The .... is an organization whose membership consists primarily of conservative evangelical Christians active in social-issue politics. (Members of other faiths may also join.)

7. The elections of 1896 and 1932 are examples of .... elections.

8. The ticket-splitting of the electorate has helped congressmen and congresswomen of the .... party.

9. The most loyal group in the Democratic voting coalition has been ....

10. The region of the United States with the lowest voter turnout for the 1972 presidential election was the ....

ANSWERS

Glossary Completion

1. straight-ticket voting
2. split-ticket voting
3. poll tax
4. primary election
5. general election
6. closed primary
7. open primary
8. visual
9. realigning election
10. PAC

Review Exercise

1. 521,000
2. 53%
3. women
4. Twenty-Sixth
5. Democratic
6. moral majority
7. critical or realigning
8. Democratic
9. blacks
10. South

8 Interest Groups

After reading and reviewing the material in this chapter, you should be able to:

1. Explain why the characteristics of American society and government encourage a multiplicity of interest groups, and compare the American and British experiences.

2. Indicate the historical conditions under which interest groups are likely to form, and specify the kinds of organizations Americans are most likely to join.

3. Describe relations between leaders and rank-and-file members of groups, indicating why the sentiments of members may not determine the actions of leaders.

4. Describe several methods that interest groups use to formulate and carry out their political objectives, especially the lobbying techniques used to gain public support. Explain why courts have become an important forum for "public interest" groups.

5. List the laws regulating conflict of interest, and describe the problems involved with "revolving door" government employment. Describe the provisions of the 1978 conflict-of-interest law. Explain the suggestions that have been made for stricter laws. Describe the balance between First Amendment freedom of expression and the need to prevent corruption in the political system.

GLOSSARY COMPLETION

1. .... interest group .... An organization (other than a political party) that seeks to influence public policy.

2. .... The mass-membership base of an organization.

3. .... An organization not financed primarily by its constituency.

4. .... Representatives of organizations that try to persuade government officials to do things.

5. .... A signal of the values at stake in an issue that government officials look for.

COMMON MISCONCEPTIONS

1. **"All major interests are represented by national associations of interest groups."**
   False. At times major segments of society, such as blacks, farmers, the poor, and migrant workers, have been unrepresented. Movements arise in response to economic conditions, and through much of American history there has been a struggle to organize those without effective representation. Frequently large numbers of constituents do not belong to the unions, civil rights organizations, or religious organizations that claim to speak in their name.

   Pages ....

2. **"Interest groups automatically give expression to the sentiments of their membership."**
   False. Leaders act according to their own perceptions at times, especially on civil rights issues and foreign policy matters. To create coalitions, they may join with other groups and espouse their causes. Groups may also take positions because of "sponsors" or donors of funds.

   Pages ....

3. **"The unorganized are completely unrepresented in American politics."**
   False. Sponsored groups may act as surrogates. Other groups may join with sponsored groups in coalitions, a situation that occurred in the early stages

of the civil rights movement. There are executive-branch agencies and members of Congress who also may take up the banner for a politically unorganized group.

Pages ....

DATA CHECK

TABLE 8.2 Political Action Committees, p. 220

1. Note that most of the ten top-spending PACs were conservative and gave disproportionately to Republicans. Only 6 and 10 could be considered liberal and leaning to Democrats.

2. Note that most of the PAC contributions went to congressional rather than to presidential campaigns. Twice as much went to House as to Senate races.

3. Consider the different spending patterns of corporate and union PACs. The unions contributed smaller amounts, but concentrated almost exclusively on Democratic incumbents. Corporate and other PACs contributed to both parties, and gave a greater proportion of their funds to contests in which no incumbent was running. What might account for the differences?

4. Note that Democrats received more funds from the PACs than Republicans. Compare this data with 1982 congressional election contributions, as reported by the FEC and printed in *The New York Times* and in *Congressional Quarterly Weekly Reports*. Was there a significant advantage for the Republicans?

5. How would you use the data in this table if someone told you that big business supports the Republicans and that its money can determine who gets elected to Congress?

STATE YOUR CASE

Some people think we need much stricter regulation of the activities of interest group lobbyists. They cite corruption, "Koreagate" scandals, and the impact of political action committees and their campaign contributions. Other people think such laws infringe on the First Amendment rights of free speech and of freedom to petition the government. Do you think interest group committees should be closely regulated by the government? Can you think of any dangers to freedom of expression that might occur?

REVIEW EXERCISE

1. Where political .... are strong, interest groups are likely to be weak.

2. The farm organization that the federal government helped to organize was the ....

3. Unions grew in size rapidly after Congress passed laws in the 19.........s.

4. Civil rights and antiwar organizations planned major demonstrations to influence government policy in the 19.........s.

5. Less than .... percent of U.S. workers belong to unions.

6. Examples of organizations that can take positions on some issues without worrying about rank-and-file opinions are .... and ....

7. By law a .... is not supposed to lobby Congress.

8. Labor groups make almost all of their contributions to members of the .... party.

9. Between 1969 and 1973, 1,406 Pentagon officials left government to take jobs in the ....

10. A law passed in 1978 bars .... from representing anyone before their former agencies in any matter in which the officials had been involved before leaving the government.

ANSWERS

Glossary Completion

1. interest group
2. rank and file
3. sponsored organization
4. lobbyists
5. cue

Review Exercise

1. parties
2. American Farm Bureau Federation
3. 1930s
4. 1960s
5. 27%
6. AFL-CIO, National Council of Churches, some unions and business groups
7. government agency
8. Democratic
9. defense industry
10. former executive-branch officials

9 The Media

After reading and reviewing the material in this chapter, you should be able to:

1. Describe the evolution of journalism in American political history, and indicate the differences between the party press and the mass media of today.

2. Demonstrate how the characteristics of the electronic media have affected the actions of public officials and candidates for national office.

3. Show the impact of the pattern of ownership and control of the media on the dissemination of news and how wire services and networks have affected national news coverage. Discuss the impact of the "national press."

4. Describe the rules that govern the media, and contrast the regulation of electronic and print media. Indicate the impact libel laws have on freedom of the press and of "fairness" rules on broadcasters.

5. Assess the impact of the media on politics, and indicate why it is so difficult to find evidence that can be used to make a meaningful and accurate assessment. Explain why the executive branch probably benefits at the expense of Congress.

6. Describe the "adversarial press" and the way in which reporters use their sources. Indicate how an administration may develop tactics to use against the adversarial press.

GLOSSARY COMPLETION

1. ....*press media*............ Term used for all means of communication.

2. ....*libel*............ Written statements that maliciously defame or ridicule an individual.

3. ....*exposé*............ News story that reveals facts previously unknown and that are of a damaging nature.

4. ....*Prime time*............ Time period from 7 P.M. to 10 or 11 P.M. on television.

5. ....*television mass appeal*............ A "look" appealing to a mass television audience.

6. ....*leak*............ Information given to a reporter by an interested source.

7. ....*adversary press*............ Members of the media inclined to be suspicious of officialdom.

COMMON MISCONCEPTIONS

1. **"Freedom of the press means that Congress cannot regulate the mass media."**
   False. Print media can be regulated as a business (antitrust laws, postal regulations, labor-management laws). Courts can apply the laws of libel and obscenity. Electronic media are regulated because they use public airwaves and are considered a public trust.

   Pages ....

2. **"The media simply act as 'messengers' that carry objective 'news.'"**
   False. Media owners are businesspeople who try to get audiences. They may choose to go after nonroutine "news" by sponsoring investigative units that will engage in exposés and muckraking. Often editors will go on "crusades" to highlight an issue of particular concern in the hope of gaining additional readers or viewers. Reporters have their own political beliefs, which may shape their perceptions of events, and columnists and editorial page writers are expected to promote their own values.

   Pages ....

3. **"Media manipulation has had a major demonstrable impact on voting behavior in most elections."**

   False. Surveys have not demonstrated a significant difference between those watching TV a great deal and those watching little during a campaign. Newspaper endorsements and editorials seem to have little impact. Advertisements provide more information than news spots; and debates, which provide even more information, do seem to have had an impact on voters in 1960 and 1976. Perhaps the greatest impact of the media is on primary campaigns, especially benefiting those who are not well known.

   Pages ....

DATA CHECK

TABLE 9.1   The Political Attitudes of the Media Elite, p. 239

1. Some observers have argued that the media elite hold very different beliefs from "middle Americans." For which questions do the media answers seem to support that case?

2. Do you think the answers to questions 1, 2, 6, and 9 are way out of line with American public opinion? On which questions do you think the divergence is greatest?

STATE YOUR CASE

Some people think that "equal time" provisions should be adhered to in presidential elections so that all parties and points of view have an equal opportunity to reach the public, especially in national debates. Others believe that such provisions should be suspended or modified so that only the two major parties—those the people most want to hear—will confront each other. What do you think? (In considering this issue, remember that the government regulates the airways, which are owned by the people. Would the government, by restricting debate to two major parties, be suppressing other opinions? Or would it merely be facilitating a meaningful debate?)

REVIEW EXERCISE

1. An example of a party press newspaper was the ....
....

2. The first newspaper telegraph service was the ....*AP*........................... ,
begun in ....*1848*............ .

3. There were competing newspapers in only ....*4*............ percent of the
U.S. cities in 1972.

4. For a paper to be found guilty of libel of a public official, one must show not
only that what was printed was inaccurate, but also that it was printed
.........*ad*............ .

5. No one may operate a television station without first obtaining a license from
the ....*FCC*..................... .

6. The ....*F*............ doctrine obliges broadcasters to present contrasting
sides of controversial public issues.

7. Local newspapers have generally endorsed candidates for president from
the .... party.

8. The source of most news for a majority of Americans in 1981 was
....

9. The most believable source of news for Americans in 1981 was
....

10. The Official Secrets Act is used to regulate the press by the government of
....

ANSWERS

Glossary Completion

1. media
2. libel
3. exposé
4. prime time

5. telegenic
6. leak
7. adversarial press

Review Exercise

1. *Gazette of the United States* or *National Gazette* or *National Intelligencer* or *Washington Globe*
2. Associated Press; 1848
3. 4%
4. maliciously
5. Federal Communications Commission

6. fairness
7. Republican
8. television
9. television
10. England

PART III

Institutions of Government

10 Congress

CHAPTER FOCUS

After reading and reviewing the material in this chapter, you should be able to:

1. Compare the essential characteristics of a parliamentary system with the characteristics of the American Congress.

2. Show how the desire of the Framers to create a system of checks and balances influenced the way they designed Congress and assigned powers to it.

3. Describe the system of strong party leadership in the House of Representatives between 1889 and 1910, and give reasons why such a system could not be maintained.

4. Assess the decline of competitiveness in congressional elections, and evaluate the impact of "careerism" on the activities of legislators, especially in constituent matters.

5. Describe the units that have gained power in Congress as the party has weakened, and specify the present power of party leaders in the decentralized structure of power.

6. Discuss the structure of the committee and subcommittee system. List the different kinds of committees, and show how decentralization and democratization have affected the structure of power in Congress.

7. Trace the steps in the legislative process by which bills become laws. Describe

and assess the contribution of the president to the legislative process. List and discuss the work of the new congressional staff agencies.

8. List and discuss the different explanations for congressional voting behavior. Indicate the circumstances in which each theory has some validity. Explain the problems with each explanation.

9. Discuss the ways in which some members of Congress have abused their office in recent years. Assess the new ethics regulations in terms of effectiveness.

GLOSSARY COMPLETION

1. .... An assembly of representatives that chooses a leader and cabinet from amongst themselves and in which the debate function is paramount.

2. .... A gathering of representatives of constituencies that legislates, supervises administration, and exercises authority independent of other branches, and in which the representation function is paramount.

3. .... Describes a two-chamber legislature.

4. .... A meeting of all legislators of the same party.

5. .... System to choose committee leaders on the basis of longest uninterrupted term of service.

6. .... Speech or speeches made for the purpose of delaying action by a legislature.

7. .... A vote to end debate on a measure before a legislature.

8. .... Districts in which the winner receives less than 55 percent of the vote.

9. .... Drawing lines for seats so that some districts have far more population than others.

10. .... Drawing lines for seats to make it easier for one party to win the district.

11. .... The honorific position of presiding officer of the Senate.

12. .... Principal leaders of the two Senate parties.

13. .... Senator whose job it is to keep party leaders informed about the views and intentions of other senators.

14. .... Presiding officer of the House of Representatives.

15. .... A vote in which a specified percentage of one party votes against a specified percentage of another party.

16. .... Committee appointed on a continuing basis with legislative duties.

17. .... Temporary committee appointed for a specific purpose.

18. .... Committee on which legislators from both Senate and House serve.

19. .... Committee to reconcile different versions of a bill prior to final passage by Congress.

20. .... Practice that permits senators to "veto" appointments made by the president in their home states.

COMMON MISCONCEPTIONS

1. **"Congress is primarily a deliberative body with members interested in debating broad policies in the national interest."**
   False. Congress has been primarily a representational body, whose members are interested in shaping national policies to meet regional, state, and district concerns, and in providing their constituents with a wide variety of goods and services.

   Pages ....

2. **"The presidency has been the dominant institution of national government since 1787."**
   False. For most of American history Congress has been the dominant institution, especially in domestic affairs. Struggles for national power have involved party or personal contests within Congress. Only since the 1930s have presidents frequently exercised substantial power in domestic affairs on a continuing basis.

   Pages ....

3. **"Members of Congress represent a cross section of the American people."**
   False. Most members have been white, middle-aged males in excess of their proportion in the population. About half have been lawyers. Members are wealthier and better educated than the average citizen.

   Pages ....

4. **"Parties dominate the activities of Congress."**
   False. No party organization, in or out of Congress, controls the members. Congressmen need not follow party leaders, and caucus decisions are rarely made on policy matters—and in any event the decisions are not binding. Often district, interest group, or other factors will be more important than party affiliation in determining how the members vote.

   Pages ....

5. **"The president dominates the legislative process by introducing most bills that Congress considers."**
   False. Most bills are private members' bills dealing with constituent or district issues. Congress introduces some major bills, and the president introduces others. Of those the president introduces some have previously been considered by Congress, often years before, so there are relatively few "new" proposals an administration sends to Congress. The staff entrepreneurs and the pooled resources of the legislative branch bring to the attention of committees many new ideas and proposals, some of which are incorporated into the presidential program.

   Pages ....

DATA CHECK

FIGURE 10.2 The Decline of Party Votes in the House of Representatives, 1897–1980, p. 272

1. The graph refers only to the percentage of votes in the House that fit either a "loose" or "strict" definition of party voting. In 1965–1967, for example, of

all the recorded votes cast in the House, in only 2% did 90% of the Democrats vote against 90% of the Republicans.

2. Note the relatively slow decline in party voting under the "loose" definition, and compare it with the decline under the "strict" definition.

3. Compare the data for 1957–1959, when a Republican president faced a Democratic Congress, with the data for 1965–1967, when a Democratic president worked with a Democratic Congress. Does split government seem to make much difference in the rate of party voting?

4. Examine the data for 1961–1969. Use these data to prove or refute the proposition that partisanship in Congress increased greatly in the Great Society and Vietnam War years.

5. Examine the data for 1969–1980. Does it provide evidence for the proposition that Carter was a far less effective legislative leader than prior presidents?

TABLE 10.1   Blacks and Women in Congress, 1947–1981

1. Note data on women in the Senate. What fact about the way women used to enter the Senate accounts for the three women in the 83rd Senate?

2. Note that progress for women in gaining election to the House has been slow. In the 84th Congress there were 16 women, in the 86th there were 17, and in the 97th only two more were added.

3. Do you find the increase of blacks in the House more or less rapid than the increase in women? (Note that the rate of growth is different for each group, depending on the date at which you start. Compare results if you start with the 90th Congress, or if you start with the 92nd Congress.)

STATE YOUR CASE

Some people believe that Congress should concentrate on legislating solely in the national interest, and that it should revamp its procedures to emphasize debate, party discipline, and responsibility. Other people believe that Congress should continue to emphasize its representational and constituency service functions, and concentrate more on administrative oversight and less on trying to make national policies (which would be left to the president). What do you think?

REVIEW EXERCISE

1. The principal work of Congress takes place in ....

2. The Framers expected that .... would be the dominant institution in the national government.

3. Efforts to decentralize power in Congress are based on the assumption that the legislature should be a .... body.

4. In the years .... strong partisan leaders controlled the House of Representatives.

5. The .... Committee determines the procedures by which bills are considered on the floor of the House.

6. For almost a century members of the Senate were chosen by ....

7. In the 1950s the typical representative served .... terms in Congress.

8. The size of the House of Representatives is determined by

9. The .... Office advises Congress on the economic effects of spending programs and on the cost of proposed policies.

10. Congress proposes amendments to the Constitution by .... resolution.

11. The .... Calendar is used in the House for bills to raise revenue or to spend money.

12. The quorum for the Committee of the Whole is .... members.

13. A bill vetoed by the president can be overridden by a vote of .... of the members present in both chambers of Congress.

ANSWERS

Glossary Completion

1. Parliament
2. Congress
3. bicameral
4. party caucus
5. seniority
6. filibuster
7. cloture
8. marginal districts
9. malapportionment
10. gerrymandering
11. president pro tempore
12. majority and minority leaders
13. whip
14. Speaker of the House
15. party vote
16. standing committee
17. select committee
18. joint committee
19. conference committee
20. senatorial courtesy

Review Exercise

1. committees
2. Congress
3. representational
4. 1889–1910
5. Rules
6. state legislatures
7. four or more
8. Congress
9. Congressional Budget
10. joint
11. Union
12. one hundred
13. two-thirds

11 The Presidency

After reading and reviewing the material in this chapter, you should be able to:

1. Compare the intentions of the Framers, especially their fears of a strong presidential office, with our own demands on the presidency. What powers have modern presidents gained? What additional responsibilities do they now have?

2. Compare presidential and parliamentary systems. What are the powers of the prime minister? Compare the American cabinet with the cabinet of a parliamentary system. In what way are the British prime minister and cabinet accountable to Parliament? What is a "vote of confidence"?

3. Consider the role of the president as legislative leader. Is he effective in leading his congressional party? What is the impact of the bicameral system? How important is his popularity in getting his program passed?

4. Consider the role of the president as administrative chief. Are all agencies under his direct control? Can he remove all officials at will?

5. Describe the major resources of the president. Do you think they are his formal powers—such as the veto, removals, and appointments—or are they leadership of his party and public opinion?

GLOSSARY COMPLETION

1. .... Head of government in a parliamentary system.

2. .... Group meeting in each state capital that casts the actual state vote for president.

3. .... Political group that favored a weak president as part of its political philosophy.

4. .... Group of offices, councils, and agencies reporting directly to the president and which performs services for him.

5. .... Heads of the major administrative departments.

6. .... Persons holding posts as deputy secretary or assistant secretary in the departments.

7. .... Persons who alternate between jobs in government and jobs in the private sector.

8. .... Power of the president to reject legislation passed by Congress.

9. .... Presidential power to block legislation by not signing a bill within ten days and Congress has adjourned within that time.

10. .... Power to withhold information from Congress or the courts, exercised by the president.

11. .... Power to disapprove of reorganization plans by concurrent resolution, exercised by Congress.

12. .... Power to remove a president from office, exercised by the Senate after a vote by the House.

COMMON MISCONCEPTIONS

1. **"The president controls Congress and it passes most of his program."**
   False. Congress generally has passed less than half of the presidential program, and of bills it passes, many have been substantially modified.

   Pages ....

2. **"The president controls all administrative agencies because he is the chief executive."**
   False. Congress may by law set up independent regulatory commissions, boards, and agencies, whose members or chairpersons are not removable by the president and whose responsibilities rest primarily in carrying out the statutes, rather than in following the priorities of the president.

   Pages ....

3. **"The cabinet serves as the principal organ of the administration in making policy."**
   False. There is no collective responsibility. Cabinet members often feud with one another, and even with the president. The president's primary advisers are members of the White House Office, the Executive Office of the President, key legislators, and people outside government.

   Pages ....

4. **"Presidents are popular leaders who can always get their way by appealing to public opinion."**
   False. Often presidents do poorly in public opinion polls, their popularity usually declines while in office, and Congress resents it when they attempt to appeal directly to the people to put pressure on the legislature. But it can be shown that the higher a president's standing in the polls, the greater proportion of his legislative proposals are approved by Congress.

   Pages ....

5. **"Presidential powers under the Constitution are absolute."**
   False. The presidential veto may be overridden. The impoundment power is regulated by legislation passed in 1974. Executive privilege may be limited by the Supreme Court. And the power of removal may be qualified when Congress creates independent agencies.

   Pages ....

6. **"Most presidents serve two terms in office."**

   False.   Between 1900 and 1981 the only presidents who served two terms or more were Wilson, Franklin Roosevelt, and Eisenhower.

   Pages ....

DATA CHECK

TABLE 11.4   Partisan Gains or Losses in Congress in Presidential Elections, p. 325

1. "Year" refers to the presidential election year, and "president" refers to the winner of the election, not necessarily to the occupant of the White House in that year.

2. The purpose of this table is to determine whether or not a party's victory in the presidential election is associated with increases in its share of House and Senate seats.

3. Compare the figures for the 1932–1948 period with the figures for 1952–1980. Has the "coattail" effect increased or decreased for the Senate? For the House?

4. Eisenhower won an overwhelming victory in 1956, and Nixon did the same in 1972. Were there any Senate coattails in those years for the Republicans? Compare with 1980.

5. Kennedy in 1960 and Carter in 1976 barely won election. Use the data in this table to support or refute the theory that members of Congress rode to victory on the coattails of Democratic presidents.

TABLE 11.5   Partisan Gains or Losses in Congress in Off-Year Elections, p. 327

1. "Year" refers to the congressional election year, and "president" refers to the incumbent in that year. A plus sign before the number means an increase in seats for the president's party, while a minus sign reflects a net loss of seats.

2. The purpose of this table is to show that the party that controls the White House loses seats in almost all off-year elections. Compare the number of pluses with the number of minuses.

3. Compare the 1934–1958 period with the 1962–1978 period. Are losses getting smaller in the Senate? Do you detect a trend in the House?

4. How would you use the data in this chart if someone told you that Carter's off-year election losses indicated that the people had lost confidence in his administration?

Figure 11.3 Presidential Popularity, p. 328

1. The line connects measurements made every few months by the Gallup Organization.

2. Note which presidents tended to remain above the 50 percent mark in popularity. Have recent presidents been more popular than those of twenty to thirty years ago?

3. Note the slight rise in popularity near the end of the Truman, Eisenhower, Johnson, and Nixon (first term) presidencies. This is known as the "rebound effect." What reasons might have kept Carter from benefitting from such an effect?

4. Consider how Reagan has fared. (Gallup polls are printed in *The Gallup Opinion Index*; it is published monthly and is available in many college libraries.)

Figure 11.4 How the President Fares in Congress, p. 338

1. The higher line refers to congressional votes that upheld the position of the president on bills, whether he introduced them or not. The lower line, the "box score," is a measurement of success on bills actually proposed by the administration.

2. What comparisons can you make among Eisenhower, Nixon, and Ford, three Republican presidents who dealt with Democratic Congresses?

3. What comparisons can you make between Kennedy and Carter, two Democrats who dealt with Democratic Congresses?

4. Use the data in this table to support or refute the proposition that a Republican president can never win much cooperation from a Democratic Congress.

STATE YOUR CASE

Some people think that the presidency has become too powerful and that it can override the checks and balances system to become "imperial." These people think that the courts, Congress, and public opinion should act to more precisely define, confine, and limit presidential powers, and that the incumbent should attempt to be more responsive to the will of Congress. Other people believe that the president is already so checked and limited that he cannot effectively lead the nation, and believe that Congress should assist the president and be more accommodating to his wishes. What do you think?

REVIEW EXERCISE

1. The president is the .... of the armed forces.

2. The president may grant .... and .... for federal offenses.

3. The .... Amendment to the Constitution limits presidents to two terms in office.

4. To be president one must be at least .... years of age and a resident of the United States for at least .... years.

5. Since 1971 the White House staff has numbered over ....

6. Franklin D. Roosevelt and Jimmy Carter—at first—used the .... method to organize their staffs in the White House Office.

7. The .... assembles the president's budget, prepares reorganization plans, and helps prepare the legislative program.

8. The Federal Reserve Board and the National Labor Relations Board are examples of .... agencies whose heads serve for .... terms of office.

9. President .... held the highest average number of press conferences per year and President .... the lowest.

10. A bill not signed or vetoed by the president within ten days while Congress is still in session will ....

11. Less than .... percent of presidential vetoes have been overridden.

12. The Supreme Court case entitled .... dealt with the doctrine of executive privilege.

13. The vice-president presides over the .... and votes in case of a ....

14. Congress may block a presidential reorganization plan by exercising a ....

ANSWERS

Glossary Completion

1. prime minister
2. Electoral College
3. Whig
4. Executive Office of the President
5. cabinet officers
6. subcabinet
7. in-and-outers
8. veto
9. pocket veto
10. executive privilege
11. legislative veto
12. impeachment

Review Exercise

1. commander-in-chief
2. reprieves; pardons
3. Twenty-Second
4. thirty-five; fourteen
5. 500
6. "circular"
7. Office of Management and Budget
8. independent; fixed
9. Franklin Roosevelt; Richard Nixon
10. become law
11. 4%
12. *United States* v. *Nixon*
13. Senate; tie
14. legislative veto

12 The Bureaucracy

CHAPTER FOCUS

After reading and reviewing the material in this chapter, you should be able to:

1. List and describe the three aspects of our constitutional system that give the bureaucracy a distributive character, and compare the situation of American officials with that of their European counterparts in parliamentary systems.

2. Describe the congressional and party constraints on presidential appointment powers, and indicate why it is often to the president's advantage to appoint the choices of others.

3. Outline the growth of the federal bureaucracy and indicate the impact of the Civil War. Contrast the size and functions of the bureaucracy today with its pre–Civil War counterpart.

4. List the various categories of government employees, and indicate the different ways they are appointed. Describe the Senior Executive Service and indicate its purpose. Show how the exempted service provides patronage opportunities for the president. Discuss the differences in job security between merit and political appointees. Define "issue network."

5. Explain how the parochialism of the highest level civil servants can affect their relations with an administration. Which seems more important in determining bureaucrats' behavior—personal attributes or the mission of the agency?

6. Explain in what ways the powers of bureaucracies can be limited or constrained in the political system, and describe the external forces with which a

government bureau must cope. What differences are there between "presidential" and "congressional" agencies? How does Congress exercise oversight over the bureaucracy?

GLOSSARY COMPLETION

1. .... A large complex organization that is composed of appointed officials and in which formal authority is divided among several managers.

2. .... Cabinet-level organizations staffed by political appointees of the president.

3. .... Appointments and favors offered on the basis of political considerations.

4. .... Authority of officials to choose courses of action and to make policies not spelled out in advance by laws.

5. .... System for appointing officials based on a civil service examination and selection criteria.

6. .... Officials not appointed on the basis of qualifications designed or approved by the Office of Personnel Management.

7. .... Jobs of a confidential or policy-determining nature below the subcabinet level.

8. .... A doctrine about the proper activity of an agency that is widely shared by its officials.

9. .... Power of congressional committees to approve certain agency actions prior to their implementation.

COMMON MISCONCEPTIONS

1. **"The bureaucracy is responsible only to the president."**
   False. In the American system the president and Congress both have constitutional authority to supervise agencies. Congress can exercise legislative

oversight based on its powers of legislation, appropriation, and the Senate responsibility to advise and consent to nominations.

Pages ....

2. **"The bureaucracies of all major Western nations do pretty much the same thing."**
False. Publicly operated enterprises account for about 12% of the employment in France and England, but less than 3% in the United States. There is far less government ownership of the economy in the United States than in comparable parliamentary democracies of Europe.

Pages ....

3. **"The size of the federal bureaucracy has increased sharply in recent years."**
False. Federal employment is about the same today as in 1970, and the federal government employs a smaller percentage of the civilian work force today than in 1955. But it is true that until recently the number of persons working for agencies largely or entirely supported by federal funding had been increasing rapidly, although such persons did not appear on a federal payroll.

Pages ....

4. **"Jobs in the bureaucracy appeal to timid, cautious, inflexible officials in love with red tape."**
False. There is no single "bureaucratic" personality. One study showed that federal executives were idealistic and achievement oriented. Other studies showed great differences in personality and behavior among different types of officials.

Pages ....

5. **"Bureaucrats see the public interest from the presidential perspective."**
False. Agencies are dominated by officials who have spent most of their careers there. Consequently, officials identify more with the mission of the agency than with the priorities of the administration.

Pages ....

6. **"Personality, background, and attitudes are decisively important in determining the behavior of officials."**
False. Key variables seem to be the missions of particular agencies, the kind of role officials assume in their jobs, and forces inside the agencies, such as government rules, the need to obtain concurrences, and statutory requirements.

Pages ....

7. **"Most agencies are more responsive to the president than to Congress."**
   False. Whether an agency is "presidential" or "congressional" depends on its outputs. A government bureau that does things that affect constituents directly by providing goods and services is likely to receive close congressional oversight and may become quite responsive to members of Congress at the expense of the administration.

   Pages ....

DATA CHECK

FIGURE 12.2   Federal Government Growth: Money, Rules, and People, p. 357

1. The vertical axis measures growth. Whatever quantities of employment, regulations, and expenditures existed in 1949 are assigned the value "100" on the chart. A doubling of those quantities in any subsequent year would receive the value "200."

2. Note that in thirty years civilian employment has hardly increased at all. In fact, it has not kept pace with the increase in population.

3. But expenditures have increased twelvefold, with the sharpest increases occurring after 1965.

4. Consider the measurement of government regulations. The quantity was measured at the value "250" in 1969 when the Republicans took over the administration. It increased to "800" in the last year of the Ford administration. What was the percentage increase under the Republicans? (Use the calculation 800 minus 250 divided by 250 to obtain your answer.)

5. Use the data in this table to support or refute the proposition that Republican presidents have cut back on "big government."

STATE YOUR CASE

Some people think that "big government" gets even bigger because officials are power hungry and eager to expand bureaucratic empires. Others think that government expansion is due to demands placed on the bureaucracies by the public, and that the problem (if it is a problem) is political rather than "bureaucratic." What do you think? (In considering your answer, you might want to focus on campus issues. Do you think most students favor or oppose cuts in government spending for dormitories, laboratories, scholarships, and research made by the Reagan administration? Do you think student attitudes are representative of American public opinion generally? Are students acting in their own interest or in the public interest? If the latter, how would you define "public interest"?

REVIEW EXERCISE

1. Government agencies in the United States operate with the prospects of judicial intervention because of our .... culture.

2. The United States relies on .... rather than ownership as the proper government approach to the economy.

3. Before the Civil War the great expansion of federal employment occurred primarily in the .... Office.

4. The modern bureaucracy was a product of the .... of the 1930s and of the .... in the 1940s.

5. About .... civilians work for the federal government.

6. Officials of the .... service are not appointed on the basis of examinations administered or approved by the Office of Personnel Management.

7. An example of an agency with a strong sense of mission is ....

8. No money may be spent by an agency unless it has first been .... and .... by Congress.

9. The right of Congress to negate certain presidential and agency decisions is known as the legislative ....

ANSWERS

Glossary Completion

1. bureaucracy
2. departments
3. patronage
4. discretionary authority
5. competitive service

6. excepted service
7. Schedule C
8. organizational mission
9. legislative veto

Review Exercise

1. adversary
2. regulation
3. Post
4. Depression; Second World War
5. 2.9 million
6. excepted

7. Forest Service, Federal Bureau of Investigation, Public Health Service
8. authorized; appropriated
9. veto

13 The Judiciary

CHAPTER FOCUS

After reading and reviewing the material in this chapter, you should be able to:

1. Describe the major concerns of the Supreme Court in the periods 1789–1865, 1865–1937, 1938 to present. Indicate the significance of the major cases discussed in the text.

2. Discuss the importance of *Marbury* v. *Madison* in extending the power of the courts in the checks and balances system. Explain how Marshall was able to assert the power of judicial review in a way that could not be defied by President Jefferson and Congress.

3. Outline the structure of the federal court system and explain its jurisdiction. Contrast the constitutional courts with the legislative courts and give examples of each. Indicate how federalism affects the structure and jurisdiction of the federal court system.

4. Evaluate the partisan influences on federal judicial appointments. Define "senatorial courtesy" and show its impact on the appointment process. Explain why the justices of the Supreme Court tend to be independent of political influences by the president once they are appointed.

5. Explain how a case moves from lower to higher courts through the appeals and certiorari systems. Explain the rules involved in "standing" and how they have changed. Describe class actions and explain their uses by groups to change public policy.

6. Discuss how courts make policy by interpreting the Constitution and the laws. Explain the rule of "stare decisis," the doctrine of "political questions," the pros and cons of judicial activism. Describe the checks on judicial power by the other branches of government.

GLOSSARY COMPLETION

1. .... The right to declare laws or actions of officials void if they conflict with the Constitution.

2. .... A judicial order requiring a public official to take an action.

3. .... An order preventing a person from doing something.

4. .... A court that exercises powers found in Article III of the Constitution.

5. .... A court that exercises powers granted originally in Article I of the Constitution.

6. .... A discretionary action of the Supreme Court to review a case of the highest state court which involves a "substantial federal question."

7. .... The right to bring suit in a court.

8. .... A case brought on behalf of all persons with similar circumstances.

9. .... The party bringing the action to court.

10. .... A brief submitted to a court from a party not immediately involved in the case.

11. .... A short unsigned opinion of a court.

12. .... The principle that cases should be settled according to principles used to decide prior similar cases.

13. .... An issue the courts will refuse to decide, leaving it to other branches to settle.

14. .... A judicial order which sets forth the actions that must be taken to correct a situation.

COMMON MISCONCEPTIONS

1. **"The Constitution explicitly gives the Supreme Court the power to declare laws of Congress null and void."**
   False. The Constitution is silent about this power. The Supreme Court itself asserted the power in the case of *Marbury* v. *Madison* and in *McCulloch* v. *Maryland,* and it has subsequently been accepted by the other branches as part of the checks and balances system.

   Pages ....

2. **"The Supreme Court has always been supportive of the rights of the disadvantaged and of minorities in American society."**
   False. Before the Civil War it decided the *Dred Scott* case against runaway slaves. After the Civil War it narrowly limited the rights of blacks under the Fourteenth Amendment, and struck down civil rights acts passed by Congress. Between 1890 and 1910 it accepted the southern states' disfranchisement of black voters. Not until the late 1930s did the Court permit substantial federal government regulation of the economy. Not until the 1950s did the Court play a major role in the civil rights movement on behalf of blacks and other minorities.

   Pages ....

3. **"The structure and jurisdiction of the federal court system is determined by the Constitution and is regulated by the Supreme Court."**
   False. The Constitution established the Supreme Court and set forth its original jurisdiction. The lower federal courts and the appeals courts are created by Congress, which determines by law the number of justices on the Supreme Court.

   Pages ....

4. **"The major way the Supreme Court makes policy is by declaring laws of Congress and actions of the president unconstitutional."**
   False. Since 1937 relatively few federal laws have been struck down, and of these, few have been significant. Only three times since the end of the Civil War has judicial review been used against a presidential action. It is the

power to construe, to interpret, and to define federal laws, rather than strike them down, that gives the Supreme Court a major role in national policy-making. (Judicial review is, however, used routinely against actions of state governments.)

Pages ....

5. **"The Supreme Court has the final say on public policies, and its decisions cannot be overturned or evaded."**
   False. Some decisions, like those involving prayer in public schools, may be evaded by some local officials. Others, such as a decision outlawing an income tax, can be overturned by constitutional amendment. Congress can remove the jurisdiction of the Court to deal with certain issues. Or it can alter the number of justices, so that the president and Senate can "pack" the Court to overturn a decision. A president can alter the composition of the Court by the appointments he makes to fill vacancies.

   Pages ....

DATA CHECK

The Government Goes on the Defensive, p. 403

1. In the bar graph note the increase in the number of civil cases involving the government. But remember that in the same time period the population increased by half, so that to keep pace the caseload might have had an expected increase to about 21,000 by 1975. Thus, the actual increase is not as dramatic as the figures indicate.

2. Although the percentage of cases in which the United States is the plaintiff has decreased, from 87% to 40%, the actual number of such cases is approximately the same. Prove this to yourself by multiplying 14,544 by .87, and compare with 31,799 multiplied by .40. Therefore, almost the entire increase in caseload between 1941 and 1975 can be accounted for by a new category of cases in which private individuals, public interest organizations, state and local governments, or private corporations are "going on the offense" and suing the government over the decisions made in federal administrative agencies.

TABLE 13.1 Characteristics of Federal District Judges Appointed by Carter and Nixon, p. 385

1. Read *down* to determine the percent of appointees with each characteristic. In each category the totals equal 100 percent. Read *across* to compare appointments of judges by Carter and Nixon with each characteristic.

2. Compare Carter appointments with Table 7.4, "Who Likes Democrats?" in Chapter 7. Did Carter reward various groups proportionately or disproportionately in making his appointments?

3. Using the same table, consider Nixon's percentage of Catholic appointees. Did that reflect the level of support given to him in 1968?

STATE YOUR CASE

Some people believe that the national judiciary must help those people who are disadvantaged politically in the system. According to this view, it should help the poor and minorities who lack effective representation in state legislatures and Congress. The courts, in this view, are the only institution that will be responsive to the demands of minorities, and therefore "judicial activism" can serve to correct injustices in American society. Other people argue that in a democracy it is up to elected officials to make social policies, and that courts have no business substituting their own notions of fairness or wisdom, especially since the justices are not elected. What do you think? (In considering this question, it may be useful to review chapters on the formation of the Union and on the Constitution, to consider whether or not the U.S. government is intended to be completely democratic.)

REVIEW EXERCISE

1. The Supreme Court can declare a law of Congress void if it is in conflict with the ....

2. The *Dred Scott* case decided that .... were not U.S. citizens.

3. After 1870 about .... state laws were declared unconstitutional.

4. Between 1887 and 1910 the Supreme Court upheld state regulations in cases involving the Fourteenth Amendment over .... percent of the time.

5. Judges of constitutional courts are nominated by the .... and confirmed by the ....

6. Controversies between two state governments are heard initially by the ....

7. About .... percent of Supreme Court cases arrive on appeal.

8. The Supreme Court rejects about .... percent of the applications for certiorari that it receives.

9. Lawsuits challenging school segregation or malapportionment of legislatures are examples of .... suits.

10. The opinion of a justice on the losing side of a case is known as the .... opinion.

11. The government is the .... in about 60 percent of the civil cases in which it is involved.

12. The House has voted to impeach a total of .... federal judges.

ANSWERS

Glossary Completion

1. judicial review
2. writ of mandamus
3. injunction
4. constitutional court
5. legislative court
6. writ of certiorari
7. standing
8. class action
9. plaintiff
10. amicus brief
11. *per curiam* opinion
12. stare decisis
13. political question
14. remedy

Review Exercise

1. Constitution
2. blacks
3. 800
4. 80%
5. president; Senate
6. Supreme Court
7. 10%
8. 99%
9. class-action
10. dissenting
11. defendant
12. 10

PART IV

The Politics of Public Policy

14 The Policy-Making Process

CHAPTER FOCUS

After reading and reviewing the material in this chapter, you should be able to:

1. Describe the processes that determine what issues get on the political agenda, and explain why the scope of legitimate governmental action has been getting larger. Pay particular attention to strategies used by interest groups, mass media, and bureaucrats.

2. Show how differences in costs and benefits of a proposed policy will affect the way in which the issue will be decided in the political process. Explain the differences between majoritarian, entrepreneurial, client, and interest group politics.

GLOSSARY COMPLETION

1. .... The results of governmental action, whether or not due to conscious policy-making.

2. .... Those issues slated to be resolved by government policy-making.

3. .... Judgments of conditions based on comparisons with others, leading to the view that one is worse off than one ought to be.

4. .... Politics of making policy where costs and benefits are widely distributed.

5. .... Politics of making policy where benefits are widely distributed and costs are highly concentrated.

6. .... Politics of making policy where benefits are concentrated and costs are widely distributed.

7. .... Politics of making policy where costs and benefits are highly concentrated.

8. .... Persons who can create legislative majorities on behalf of interests not directly represented in the government.

COMMON MISCONCEPTIONS

1. **"Policy-making always operates the same way—if you know how institutions work, you know how policies are shaped."**
   False. A key factor is the pattern of costs and benefits. The typology in this chapter is important because it shows you that different kinds of policies are associated with different decision-making techniques and because different policies have different consequences for the way institutions operate.

   Pages ....

2. **"Political controversy turns exclusively on what government should be doing."**
   False. Major controversies occur in the American system over the legitimacy of the level of government performing the activity: often people argue that the states should be doing what the federal government is doing—or vice versa. In general, the scope of legitimate governmental action has been increasing—but so have the questions about which level of government would be most effective in handling the jobs.

   Pages ....

3. **"Bureaucracy simply executes the laws and policies decided upon by entrepreneurs and politicians."**
   False. The "professionalization of reform" means that bureaucrats may make their own proposals for policy—proposals that usually would add to their responsibilities. Then officials may "sell" these ideas to the media, elected politicians, and policy entrepreneurs. Examples include some of the Great Society programs of the 1960s.

   Pages ....

4. **"The press only reports news that has happened."**
   False. The press plays a role in getting issues on the political agenda, by playing up certain stories, by investigative reporting, and by inducing legislators to take actions in response to its initiatives.

   Pages ....

REVIEW EXERCISE

1. Desegregation at Little Rock was an example of a policy originally set by the .... branch.

2. Much of the 1960s Great Society was promoted by officials of the .... branch.

3. Majoritarian politics involves costs that are .... and benefits that are ....

4. Interest group politics involves costs that are .... and benefits that are ....

5. Client politics involves costs that are .... and benefits that are ....

6. Entrepreneurial politics involves costs that are .... and benefits that are ....

7. A tariff is an example of .... politics.

8. Shipping companies and maritime unions are involved in
.... politics.

9. Requiring antipollution devices on automobiles is an example of
.... politics.

10. Ralph Nader is an example of a policy ....

ANSWERS

Glossary Completion

1. outcomes
2. political agenda
3. relative deprivation
4. majoritarian

5. entrepreneurial
6. client
7. interest group
8. policy entrepreneurs

Review Exercise

1. judicial
2. executive
3. distributed; distributed
4. concentrated; distributed
5. distributed; concentrated

6. concentrated; concentrated
7. entrepreneur
8. client
9. entrepreneurial
10. interest group

15 Business Regulation

CHAPTER FOCUS

After reading and reviewing the material in this chapter, you should be able to:

1. Define client politics, indicate the type of relationship that occurs between government and business, and offer some historical examples of how regulatory agencies have benefited organized interest groups.

2. Explain why client politics may sometimes involve corruption of public officials, and offer an example.

3. Define interest group politics, indicate the type of relationship that occurs between government and business, and offer some examples of struggles involving rival interest groups.

4. Define majoritarian politics and explain why the Sherman Act and the Clayton Act fit into this category.

5. Define entrepreneurial politics and discuss the strategy that might be used to enact legislation when a bill can be expected to have strong interest group opposition and little or no interest group support.

6. List some of the problems deregulation creates for industries and government. Explain why some sectors of the economy may resist deregulation.

GLOSSARY COMPLETION

1. .... Agency that regulates union-organizing drives and hears complaints of unfair labor practices.

2. .... Law that makes illegal the closed shop and secondary boycotts.

3. .... Law enacted in 1890 making monopolies and restraint of trade illegal.

4. .... Law enacted in 1906 that barred from interstate commerce misbranded and adulterated goods.

5. .... Agency created in 1934 to regulate the stock markets.

COMMON MISCONCEPTIONS

1. **"Big corporate interests always determine what the government does."**
False. Depending on the type of public policy (outlined in Chapter 14), business relations with government will take one of several different forms. While it is often the case that business interests will get things they want from the government, it is also often the case that they will be taxed, regulated, or required to conform to actions that they oppose.

Pages ....

2. **"Government regulation is always opposed by industry."**
False. Sometimes economic sectors prefer regulation. At times, it is intended to benefit them, especially by regulating or restricting free market competition or by offering subsidies in the form of regulatory requirements that work to their advantage.

Pages ....

3. **"Interest group struggles are resolved when Congress passes a law on the subject."**
False. The struggles are then continued in the bureaucracies that administer the laws and in the courts that interpret the laws. Interest groups will then attempt to see that their own interpretations are embodied in the regulations issued by agencies. They will try to win agency appointments for people who are sympathetic to their position.

Pages ....

4. **"Laws determine government policies."**

False.   Laws are not self-executing, and some laws may not be enforced effectively because politicians do not wish to enforce them. Consider anti-trust enforcement. In the 1890s no more than two cases were brought a year, in a period of great trust-building activity. After 1938 over fifty cases were brought each year.

Pages ....

5. **"Laws always place government regulatory agencies in a position of power over interest groups."**

False.   Laws may actually prohibit regulatory agencies from taking certain actions, and may require them to serve groups or give them preferences. Some laws require that interest groups be given a role in making public policy, or even a "veto" on policies. Laws may give interest groups power over agencies.

Pages ....

6. **"Government deregulation is always supported by industry."**

False.   Sometimes industries oppose deregulation because they benefit from existing rules or rate structures. Examples include commercial aviation and the trucking industry.

Pages ....

STATE YOUR CASE

Some people think that only majoritarian policies are in the public interest in the area of business regulation. What types of policies do you think are most likely to produce a beneficial outcome for the nation? (In considering this question, remember to include considerations of foreign policy, such as the protection of our export markets and the fierce competition for our own markets from foreign business corporations.)

REVIEW EXERCISE

1. To the political theorist ...., the state was nothing more than the executive committee of the propertied classes.

2. The law that determines the minimum price level for milk is an example of .... politics.

3. The regulation of .... by the CAB was ended by the Airline Deregulation Act of 1978.

4. Presidents from the .... party have tended to appoint management people to the NLRB.

5. The Occupational Safety and Health Act is an example of .... politics.

6. According to historian Gabriel Kolko, the .... Commission was set up to protect the railroads.

7. In a twenty-five-year span, from about 1890 to 1915, broadly based criticism of business monopolies resulted in three major pieces of .... legislation.

8. Ralph Nader is a person very effective in .... politics.

9. The oil industry has ....deregulation, while the dairy industry .... it.

ANSWERS

Glossary Completion

1. National Labor Relations Board
2. Taft-Hartley
3. Sherman Act
4. Pure Food and Drug Act
5. Securities and Exchange Commission

Review Exercise

1. Marx
2. client
3. air fares
4. Republican
5. interest group
6. Interstate Commerce
7. antitrust
8. entrepreneurial
9. favored, opposed

16 Economic Policy

CHAPTER FOCUS

After reading and reviewing the material in this chapter, you should be able to:

1. Explain why the condition of the national economy is an example of majoritarian politics and discuss the ways in which perceptions of the economy can play a role in voting behavior.

2. Describe the relationship between economic ideologies and majoritarian politics. Describe the cleavages between Democrats and Republicans and between mass and elite opinion.

3. Describe the four major theories about how to manage the economy. Indicate which are favored by conservatives, which by liberals, and why.

4. Assess the effect of uncertainty on the utility of these theories, and the effects of uncertainty on government policymakers.

5. Explain how politicians in the United States attempt to stimulate the economy, especially around the election cycle.

6. Describe the four main elements of the Reagan economic program, and explain how the program differs from that of his predecessors.

7. Describe the institutional machinery by which the federal government makes economic policy. Discuss relationships within the "troika", and the problems the president has with the Federal Reserve Board.

8. Explain the advantages for governmental budgeting of the procedures instituted by the Budget Reform Act of 1974. Explain how the Reagan administration used the reconciliation procedure to advance its budgetary goals.

GLOSSARY COMPLETION

1. .... An economist who believes in increasing the money supply at a rate equal to the increase in economic productivity.

2. .... An economist who believes in activist government intervention in the economy to manage demand and influence the market.

3. .... Economists who favor large cuts in personal and business taxes to encourage additional work and investment in the private sector.

4. .... An exception, exclusion, or deduction permitted by the tax laws.

5. .... The attempt to use taxes and expenditures to affect the economy.

6. .... Use of the amount of money and the price of money to affect the economy.

7. .... A bill passed by Congress which provides funds for government agencies.

8. .... Contracts and commitments already made, payments to individuals guaranteed by law, and debt payments.

COMMON MISCONCEPTIONS

1. **"The way people vote for candidates is determined primarily by their own personal economic situation."**
   False. Most people are employed, yet surveys have shown that when unemployment is high, most employed Americans will list fighting unemployment as the top economic priority. Other studies have shown that people's

perception of the overall national economy is a better clue as to how they will vote than the changes in their own situation.

Pages ....

2. **"Public opinion and the two parties always reflect deep divisions on economic goals."**
False. There are some class and partisan divisions, but often large majorities from all classes and parties agree on priorities. This is generally the case when severe inflation occurs. The parties then are likely to disagree on means rather than on ends.

Pages ....

3. **"Politicians have little effect on economic conditions no matter what policies they pursue."**
False. Politicians have been quite effective in stimulating the economy in election years. Real disposable income in a majority of democratic nations increases faster in election years than in nonelection years, and the unemployment rates tend to decline by an average of one point in election years.

Pages ....

4. **"The president determines the levels of spending and taxing."**
False. The presidential budget is merely a recommendation to Congress, which then passes the two budget resolutions and the various tax, appropriations, and debt laws. The Congress may give the president most of what he wants, but it also can make significant changes.

Pages ....

DATA CHECK

FIGURE 16.1 Federal Outlays as a Percentage of Gross National Product, 1869–1975, p. 449

1. This figure presents a time series of outlays expressed, not in absolute terms, but as a percentage of GNP.

2. Since the GNP in most of these years was increasing, even a constant percentage would lead to an increase in actual expenditures by the government.

3. Alternatively, a decline in the percentages from one decade to the next might mask the fact that actual expenditures had increased: the government spent far more in the 1960s than in the 1940s, for example.

4. Note the sharp jumps in percentages that occurred for the two world wars and the somewhat smaller jump for the Depression of the 1930s. Was there

anything similar for the Korean War in the 1950s and the Vietnam War of the 1960s?

5. How would you use the data in this table to support or refute the proposition that with the rise of the modern welfare state there is an inexorable increase in the growth of the public sector relative to the private sector?

DATA CHECK

TABLE 16.3 Votes in Congress, by Party, on President Reagan's Tax and Spending Cuts, 1981, p. 460

1. The Democrats are divided into the northern and southern wings. Note the difference in voting behavior in the House between the two groups. Which wing gives more support to the President's position?

2. In the Senate both wings of the Democratic party supported the President's position. Why would northern Democratic Senators differ so sharply from their colleagues in the House?

3. Why would a greater percentage of Senators support the President than members of the House? Did this remain the case in the subsequent years of the Reagan administration?

4. Note how few Republicans voted against the President's program in 1981. Compare the data in this table with the strong reluctance on the part of many Republicans to support all of the Reagan economic program in subsequent years.

5. Using the data from this table, how would you respond to the argument that a popular president can rely on uniting the members of his own party in order to pass his economic program? Can a president rely solely on a partisan strategy?

STATE YOUR CASE

Some people think economic policy-making is so complicated that it is best left to expert economists. Others believe that economists use information that is so imperfect and rely on theories that are of so little use that the president should rely primarily on his own political instincts and make economic policies that will most benefit him and his party. What do you think? Is economic policy-making too important to be left to the economists? Should the president be a politician first and an "economist" second?

REVIEW EXERCISE

1. Of the two—inflation and unemployment—higher-income persons and retired persons tend to worry more about ....

2. The .... school of economists relies on the ability of government to time its efforts to stabilize the economy effectively.

3. Most tax loopholes benefit .... rather than corporations.

4. .... policy involves buying and selling federal securities and changing the interest charged to banks when they borrow from the ....

5. The .... Committee buys and sells government securities and directly affects the money supply.

6. Monetary policy is chiefly designed and carried out by the .... Board.

7. In a presidential election year the rate of .... tends to decline.

8. When .... are in office, they emphasize policies aimed at curbing inflation before reducing unemployment.

9. In the spring Congress sets a tentative ceiling on total expenditures in the .... resolution.

10. The federal government spends .... percent of the gross national product.

ANSWERS

Glossary Completion

1. monetarist
2. Keynesian
3. supply-siders
4. tax loophole

5. fiscal policy
6. monetary policy
7. appropriation
8. uncontrollable expenditures

Review Exercise

1. inflation
2. Keynesian
3. individuals
4. Monetary; Federal Reserve
5. Open Market

6. Federal Reserve
7. unemployment
8. Republicans
9. first budget
10. 20%

17 Social Welfare

After reading and reviewing the material in this chapter, you should be able to:

1. Describe the goals of the American social welfare system, and contrast its programs with those of the British in terms of centralization.

2. Describe the major elements of the American system, including the Social Security Act of 1935, the Economic Opportunity Act of 1964, and the Medicare Act of 1965. Why did these acts pass while the Family Assistance Plan of 1969 failed? What generalizations can you make about welfare politics?

3. Explain why some welfare policies can be considered majoritarian and others considered client politics. Give examples for each and indicate the political consequences.

GLOSSARY COMPLETION

1. .... Law providing social insurance for the unemployed and the elderly and supported by deductions from payroll taxes.

2. .... Law instituting training for the hard-core un-employed, literacy programs, and community action programs.

3. .... Program intended to create grass-roots partici-pation in planning and implementing service programs.

4. .... Law providing medical assistance for the poor and elderly.

5. .... A bill that proposed to aid families with de-pendent children by instituting what was in ef-fect a negative income tax.

COMMON MISCONCEPTIONS

1. **"Welfare policies are instituted primarily to redistribute income among classes."**
   False. After-tax income of all social classes is hardly changed as a propor-tion of the national income. The poor receive welfare not because they are poor but rather on the basis of certain specific disabilities or circumstances: blindness, disability, age, families with dependent children.

   Pages ....

2. **"The United States has led the way in pioneering social programs."**
   False. The United States has lagged behind other nations in passing social laws. Even today the welfare and medical programs of the United States have fewer benefits and less coverage than those of most nations of Western Europe, Canada, Australia, and Japan.

   Pages ....

3. **"The national government is responsible for social welfare administra-tion."**
   False. The major programs are decentralized with states paying some of the costs, setting some of the policies, and administering most of the pro-grams. The major exceptions, in which the national government runs the entire program, are the social security program and welfare payments to the elderly, blind, and disabled.

   Pages ....

DATA CHECK

Attitudes Toward Welfare, p. 478

1. In the Harris Survey note which questions support the concept of welfare, and which show public support for a tightening up of the system.

2. Do the answers to these questions indicate to you that people want to abolish the welfare system, or do people want to reform it?

3. How would you use the data here if someone told you that the public was fed up with red tape and wanted a guaranteed minimum-income system to restore dignity to welfare recipients?

4. The first two questions of the New York Times/CBS Poll indicate a lack of general support for welfare as an idea. But overwhelming majorities support specific welfare programs or proposals, as indicated by the answers to the last five questions.

5. Note that public support for a national health care program is high, even though it has not been enacted into law. Might this prove a problem for a president and Congress who are committed to retrenchment and fiscal austerity?

6. This survey uses 1977 data. How would you use the data if someone told you that the so-called "swing to the right" meant that public support for a government role in welfare and health services had ended in the 1970s?

TABLE 17.2 Increasing Social Welfare Spending, p. 481

1. The first column should be adjusted for inflation. Using 1978 dollars, the figure in 1970 might be equivalent to $115 billion, the 1965 figure might be $55 billion, the 1960 figure $40 billion, and the 1950 figure $25 billion. Even when adjusted to "constant 1978 dollars" what can you say about the growth of expenditures?

2. The second column refers to percentage of federal outlays and the third column refers to percentage of gross national product. Be sure you understand these terms, or ask your instructor to explain them.

3. Compare the 1960–1970 period, in which, for the most part, Democrats controlled the White House, with the 1970–1977 period of Republican control. How would you use the data in this table if someone told you that Democratic administrations, unlike their Republican counterparts, increased spending dramatically for social welfare programs?

STATE YOUR CASE

Some people think that the government should provide a guaranteed minimum income or even a negative income-tax payment to those whose income falls below the poverty line. But the majority of Americans think that these ideas go in the wrong direction. They would continue welfare for specific categories, tighten up regulations to prevent abuse, and require all able-bodied recipients to enroll in "workfare" programs. Without discussing the merits of these proposals, do you think social welfare policy should always follow the will of the majority? If not, what other criteria might be used in making decisions? (In considering this issue, how would you feel if a majority decided that all welfare payments should be eliminated? Would you go along with that?)

REVIEW EXERCISE

1. The British instituted .... legislation around the turn of the century.

2. The United States instituted social welfare legislation in the 1930s in response to the ....

3. Of the programs comprising the Social Security Act of 1935, all but .... were administered by the states.

4. The War on Poverty was declared by President ....

5. The Economic Opportunity Act was originated by the .... party.

6. Passage of the Medicare Act was long delayed by ...., chairman of the House .... Committee.

7. President .... and his urban affairs adviser, ..., created the Family Assistance Plan.

8. Debate on welfare policies tends to be .... and .... in nature.

9. .... have often allied with Republicans in Congress in voting against social welfare legislation.

10. The Medicare and Social Security Acts were examples of .... politics.

ANSWERS

Glossary Completion

1. Social Security Act
2. Economic Opportunity Act
3. Community Action Program
4. Medicare Act
5. Family Assistance Plan

Review Exercise

1. social welfare
2. Depression
3. Old Age and Survivors Disability Insurance
4. Johnson
5. Democratic
6. Wilbur Mills; Ways and Means
7. Nixon; Moynihan
8. partisan; ideological
9. Southern Democrats
10. majoritarian

18 Civil Liberties

CHAPTER FOCUS

After reading and reviewing the material in this chapter, you should be able to:

1. Discuss the relationship of the Bill of Rights to the concept of democratic rule of the majority, and give examples of tension between majority rule and minority rights. Explain how the politics of civil liberties may at times become a mass issue, and offer several examples.

2. Describe the conflicts that have arisen between those who claim First Amendment rights and those who are in favor of sedition laws that might restrict freedom of speech. Explain how the Court attempts to balance competing interests. Describe the various "tests" that the Court has applied.

3. Explain how the structure of the federal system affects the application of the Bill of Rights. How has the Court used the Fourteenth Amendment to expand coverage in the federal system? Describe the incorporation doctrine and indicate how the Court has applied it. Discuss changing conceptions of the due process clause of the Fourteenth Amendment.

4. List the categories under which the Supreme Court may classify "speech." Explain the distinction between "protected" and "unprotected" speech. What are the various forms of expression that are not protected under the First Amendment? Describe the test used by the Court to decide the circumstances under which freedom of expression may be qualified.

5. Describe what the Supreme Court decided in *Miranda* v. *Arizona,* and ex-

plain why that case illustrates how the Court operates in most such due process cases.

6. Analyze reasons why the resolution of civil liberties issues involves "politics" as well as "law." Discuss political factors that influence the Court when it decides fundamental civil liberties issues.

GLOSSARY COMPLETION

1. .... Law that made it illegal to libel the federal government.

2. .... Wartime measure that defined as criminal activities involving speech and which was spurred by the "red scare."

3. .... Law that required the Communist party to register its membership and which barred party members from holding federal appointive office.

4. .... Referring to the priority of freedom of expression over other civil liberties.

5. .... Referring to the insistence of the courts that restriction of expression involve the minimum necessary regulation.

6. .... Law that denied the Communist party the legal rights of a political party.

COMMON MISCONCEPTIONS

1. **"Civil rights are a clear standard that can be fully enforced at all times to protect minorities."**
   False. Often rights compete, and to enforce the rights of one group may deny rights to others. Examples include: the right to privacy vs. freedom of the press; freedom of speech vs. preservation of public order; "right to life" vs. "freedom of choice" in abortion cases; the rights of defendants in criminal trials vs. the rights of reporters to shield their sources in investigations.

   Pages ....

2. **"The Vietnam War was accompanied by major efforts unparalleled in American history to restrict freedom of speech and dissent."**

   False. There was no Sedition Act, no new espionage laws, no new version of the Smith Act, and less demagoguery than that exhibited by Senator Joseph McCarthy in the 1950s. Even the Subversive Activities Control Board became defunct in 1973. Between 1954 and 1974 the proportion of people willing to let Communists speak almost doubled. The end of the war brought no "red scare" or "witchhunt" of those who had opposed the war. It is true that the Justice Department did try to impose prior censorship on the *New York Times* to prevent it from printing the Pentagon Papers, but the Nixon administration was overruled by the Supreme Court.

   Pages ....

3. **"All of the Bill of Rights applies to state officials."**

   False. The Bill of Rights originally applied only to national officials. Then several rights were "incorporated" by the Court into the Fourteenth Amendment due process clause, to protect citizens against certain acts of state officials. "Activist" courts have expanded the list of actions prohibited under the due process clause, while judges practicing "judicial conservatism" will have consolidated or cut back on protections. Individuals are protected not only by the Bill of Rights but also by state constitutions, which contain their own bills of rights.

   Pages ....

DATA CHECK

TABLE 18.1 Willingness to Grant First Amendment Rights, p. 498

1. The data are arranged to indicate the support that different kinds of people give to certain First Amendment rights.

2. The table can be read in three ways: (a) *Vertically, to show differences over time in rights the public would grant.* Thus, in 1954 fewer people would let a Communist teach (6%) than speak (27%). (b) *Vertically, to show how support for rights has changed between 1954 and 1972.* Thus, in 1954, 33% would let someone advocating government ownership of industry teach in a college, while 57% would grant that right in 1974. (c) *Horizontally, to compare public tolerance of different viewpoints.* In 1974 more people were willing to grant rights to those advocating public ownership than to Communists.

3. Support or refute the proposition that you can always rely on public opinion to protect the rights of unpopular groups in a democracy.

STATE YOUR CASE

Some people think that the majority should decide, through their elected representatives, questions involving civil rights, so as to let elected officials, rather than appointed judges, make the final decisions. Others believe that the majority will discriminate against racial, religious, cultural, or political minorities, and therefore the courts must check the elected officials and enforce a set of protections guaranteed by the Constitution. Which do you think is more important: protection of minority rights or rule of the majority? (In considering this question, try to establish a "rule" that would enable you to set a boundary to distinguish between subjects that require protection for minorities and subjects in which majority rule should apply.)

REVIEW EXERCISE

1. The .... was added to the Constitution shortly after ratification.

2. Civil liberties can become a case of .... politics when a real or imagined threat to widely shared values is dramatized to mobilize a temporary majority.

3. In the case of the Sedition Act of 1798, the war against ....
   .... provided the emotional backdrop.

4. The .... party introduced the Sedition Act of 1798.

5. In 1917 fear of the Germans, Russians, and domestic Communists spurred enactment of the ....

6. In the 1920s the Supreme Court upheld convictions of pamphleteers in spite of the .... test offered by Justices .... and ....

7. According to the .... Act, speech was to be judged by its intention, and not by content alone.

8. In the .... case the Supreme Court decided that the Smith Act did not violate the First Amendment.

9. The decision of the Supreme Court in the .... case made

further prosecution under the advocacy clause of the Smith Act all but impossible.

10. In 1833 the Supreme Court ruled that the Bill of Rights applied only to actions of the .... government.

11. The Supreme Court has held that money expended to support political candidates is a form of speech and is therefore protected by the .... Amendment, but libel against private persons is not protected.

12. In 1978 the Supreme Court decided that .... have the right to free speech.

13. Under the .... rule, evidence unconstitutionally obtained can be barred from a trial.

ANSWERS

Glossary Completion

1. Sedition Act of 1798
2. Espionage Act of 1917
3. Internal Security Act of 1950
4. preferred position
5. least means
6. Communist Control Act of 1954

Review Exercise

1. Bill of Rights
2. entrepreneurial
3. France
4. Federalist
5. Espionage Act
6. clear and present danger; Holmes; Brandeis
7. Smith
8. *Dennis*
9. *Yates*
10. federal
11. First
12. corporations
13. exclusionary or Miranda

19 Civil Rights

After reading and reviewing the material in this chapter, you should be able to:

1. Contrast the experience of economic interest groups with that of black groups in obtaining satisfaction of their interests from the government. Indicate why in most circumstances the black movement involved interest group rather than client politics. Describe the strategies used by black leaders to overcome their political weaknesses, and explain why the civil rights movement has become more conventional in its strategy in recent years.

2. Summarize the legal struggles of blacks to secure rights under the Fourteenth Amendment, and indicate how the Court construed that amendment in the *Civil Rights Cases* and in *Plessy* v. *Ferguson*. Discuss the NAACP strategy of litigation, and indicate why it was suited to the political circumstances. Summarize the holdings in *Brown* v. *Board of Education* and compare with *Plessy* v. *Ferguson*.

3. Discuss the attempts to implement *Brown*. Explain why the South pursued a strategy of massive resistance, and show the consequences for implementation of *Brown*. Explain why "massive resistance" was ultimately a futile exercise for southern state politicians.

4. Discuss the rationale used by the Supreme Court in ordering busing to achieve desegregation. Explain the apparent inconsistency between *Brown* and *Charlotte-Mecklenburg*. Indicate why these decisions are not inconsistent,

and explain why the courts chose busing as an equitable remedy to deal with de jure segregation.

5. Trace the campaign launched by blacks for a set of civil rights laws. Explain why nonviolent techniques were used. Discuss the conflict between the agenda-setting and coalition-building aspects of the movement. Demonstrate how civil rights advocates could overcome sources of resistance in Congress.

6. Summarize the actions taken by Congress and by the Supreme Court since 1970. List the actions the two branches have taken to reduce the impact of court-ordered busing, or to reduce the impact of preferential treatment and affirmative action in higher education.

7. Describe the differences between the black movement and the women's movement. Indicate the various standards used by the courts in interpreting the 14th Amendment, and how these standards differ, depending on whether blacks or women are involved.

8. Explain why ratification of the Equal Rights Amendment has run into such difficulty.

GLOSSARY COMPLETION

1. .... Amendment ratified in 1868 that provided equal protection of the law for citizens.

2. .... Decisions of the Supreme Court which indicated that equal-protection clause applied only to state (and not to private) discrimination.

3. .... Case in which "separate-but-equal" doctrine was developed in interstate transportation.

4. .... Civil rights organization founded in 1909 that attacked segregation through the courts.

5. .... Cases in which the Supreme Court decided that
.... separate facilities for blacks in law schools were not equal.

6. .... Case in which the Supreme Court found "separate-but-equal" to be unconstitutional in the area of education.

7. .... System of segregation maintained by law.

8. .... System of segregation maintained by factors other than formal laws.

9. .... Refusal to strike down state laws on the grounds that women differed from men in ways that justified differences in legal status.

COMMON MISCONCEPTIONS

1. **"The judiciary has always protected the rights of blacks."**

   False. In the nineteenth century the Supreme Court upheld fugitive slave laws in the *Dred Scott* decision. After the war it struck down the Civil Rights Act and upheld the doctrine of "separate-but-equal" facilities, reinforcing state segregation. Only in the period after *Brown* was decided in the 1950s did the courts consistently play an activist role in dismantling state-legislated segregation.

   Pages ....

2. **"Brown rested solely on psychological data which indicated that blacks who were segregated felt inferior, and therefore their education suffered."**

   False. Although such a finding was used by the Court, the case also rested on the constitutional argument that to segregate people on the basis of race was *inherently* unequal and violated the Fourteenth Amendment. Even if blacks had felt superior in racially segregated situations, such state-sponsored segregation would have been unconstitutional.

   Pages ....

3. **"The Supreme Court has had the full cooperation of Congress in implementing its decisions."**

   False. Congress has limited or prohibited the use of federal funds to implement court-ordered busing decisions, and has defined "desegregation" in a way that has attempted (thus far unsuccessfully) to limit the reach of court decisions.

   Pages ....

4. **"Violent tactics have irreparably harmed and retarded the black struggle for civil rights."**

   False. It was never a strategy of the movement to use violence. It was the use of nonviolent demonstrations, designed to provoke violence from white-supremacist law-enforcement officials, that catalyzed public opinion and convinced many Americans that the time to put an end to segregation was at hand. In the last thirty years support for integration in schools, housing, and transportation has increased dramatically among whites.

Pages ....

5. **"Most presidents have been staunch supporters of the goals of the civil rights movements."**

False. Hayes was a supporter of southern whites who were attempting to remove black officials from state governments in the aftermath of Reconstruction. Wilson introduced segregation in federal employment to Washington, D.C. Franklin Roosevelt took no action during the Depression to desegregate public facilities or to provide New Deal programs on an integrated basis. Eisenhower seemed to oppose the decision to integrate public schools, although he did enforce the court order at Little Rock, Arkansas, in 1957 in a major test of national authority versus states' rights. Kennedy took several actions to reduce segregation in federally assisted public housing, but it took public pressure to induce him to introduce his civil rights bill. Lyndon Johnson, a Southerner, was the first president to identify with the black movement, and during his administration two civil rights bills and a voting rights bill were passed. Nixon claimed to favor desegregation, but opposed court-ordered busing of children to overcome racial imbalance, as has Reagan.

Pages ....

DATA CHECK

FIGURE 19.1 The Increasing Acceptance of Integrationist Beliefs, 1963–1976, p. 528

1. The bars show the percentage of respondents who answered "Same" to question 1, "Little or no objection" to question 2, "No right" to question 3, "No law" to question 4, and disagreed with statement number 5.

2. Since respondents also answered "No opinion" or "Don't know," you should *not* assume that "anti-integration" percentages can be obtained by subtracting the "pro-integration" position from 100%.

3. Note that the general trend has been toward more support of integration, but in question 1 there was less support for integration in 1976 than in 1972. What might account for this change?

4. Use the data in this figure to support or refute the proposition that was offered in the Kerner Commission report of 1968 that "America is rapidly moving toward two societies, one black and one white."

TABLE 19.2 Votes in Congress on Passage of Major Civil Rights Bills, 1957–1970, p. 534

1. The table indicates votes to pass (yes) or defeat (no) civil rights acts. The votes are classified into northern and southern Democrats and Republicans in the House and Senate.

2. There are two ways to use the data. Reading across, you can compare different groups' support for each bill. Note that the most support comes from northern Democrats, and the least support from southern Democrats. Reading down, you can see changes in the support scores in each group on successive bills. Note that initially Republicans in the House voted strongly for civil rights bills, but the 1968 Civil Rights Act and the 1970 Voting Rights Act had a substantial number of Republicans opposed.

3. Contrast House and Senate Republicans. Most Republican senators voted for civil rights bills. Can you think of any reason to account for the difference with their colleagues in the House?

4. Use the data in this table to support or refute the propositions that (1) southern Democrats are implacable foes of civil rights laws and that (2) Republicans have responded to their almost entirely white constituencies in voting on civil rights measures.

STATE YOUR CASE

Some people think that the Constitution should be color-blind, and should prohibit officials from taking race into account in any action of government. Others believe that to overcome the effects of past racial segregation which existed under official sanction, courts should be permitted to use the power of "equitable remedy" in order to consider race as a factor in ending the effects of racial segregation. What do you think? Are you opposed to or in favor of such court-ordered tools as busing and affirmative action to overcome racial segregation? What reasons can you offer for expanding or limiting the power of the courts to consider past history of racial discrimination in their decisions?

REVIEW EXERCISE

1. Much of civil rights politics can be characterized as .... politics rather than client politics.

2. As late as the year .... most southern whites opposed integrated public transportation.

3. By shifting key decisions from Congress to the ...., causes of the civil rights movement were furthered.

4. State laws that required the segregation of blacks became known as .... laws.

5. In the North de .... segregation resulted from the pattern of housing and manipulation of school boundaries.

6. In the late 1960s the Court ordered an end to .... imbalance in schools, to be achieved through means such as court-ordered ....

7. Early civil rights demonstrations based on the philosophy of nonviolent civil disobedience were led by the Reverend ....

8. By law, Congress has barred female soldiers from ....

ANSWERS

Glossary Completion

1. Fourteenth
2. *Civil Rights Cases*
3. *Plessy* v. *Ferguson*
4. NAACP
5. *Sweatt* and *McLaurin* cases

6. *Brown* v. *Board of Education*
7. de jure
8. de facto
9. protective paternalism

Review Exercise

1. interest group
2. 1956
3. courts
4. Jim Crow

5. facto
6. racial; busing
7. Martin Luther King, Jr.
8. combat

20 Foreign Policy

After reading and reviewing the material in this chapter, you should be able to:

1. List the constitutional powers of the president and compare them to the authority of Congress in foreign affairs. Indicate why it is naive to read the Constitution literally to determine which institution has the major responsibility to conduct foreign policy. Explain why the president has a larger role than the Framers intended.

2. Compare the president's powers with those of a prime minister in a parliamentary system.

3. Explain why checks on the powers of the national government in foreign affairs are primarily political rather than constitutional.

4. Give reasons for the volatility of public opinion in foreign affairs. Explain the advantages that the president obtains when he acts resolutely in crises. Describe the problems that the president may face, using public opinion on the Vietnam War as an example.

5. Explain the "world view" concept, and describe the containment strategy of Mr. X. Summarize essential elements of the Munich–Pearl Harbor and post-Vietnam paradigms. Discuss the revisionist argument that it is the material interests of elites, rather than their principles, that explain American foreign policy. Indicate the objections that may exist to this view.

6. Describe some of the problems for the President in dealing with the bureaucracies charged with managing foreign policy.

GLOSSARY COMPLETION

1. .... Belief that Americans should refrain from involvement in world affairs.

2. .... Law that requires the president to consult with Congress and report to it when sending troops into hostilities.

3. .... Strategy of thwarting every instance of Soviet expansionism; proposed in 1947 by Mr. X.

4. .... Diplomat identified with strategy of containment.

5. .... Strategy used by the British and French in dealing with Hitler's expansionism in the 1930s.

6. .... Theory that if Vietnam became a Communist state, all other countries in Southeast Asia would "fall" to communism.

COMMON MISCONCEPTIONS

1. **"The Constitution gives the president the major role in foreign affairs."**
False. The president is given the title of commander-in-chief, receives ambassadors, and shares power to nominate ambassadors to foreign countries and negotiate treaties with the Senate. But Congress has the power to regulate foreign commerce and declare war, and has powers of appropriation and legislation in foreign affairs. In fact, the Constitution gives Congress more specific powers in foreign affairs than it gives to the president.

   Pages ....

2. **"Since the public always 'rallies round the flag' in crises, the president has great freedom of action to do whatever he wants in international affairs."**
False. Such an effect occurs immediately after an international crisis. Support tends to erode if the crisis is not resolved quickly (Iran), if there is a stalemate (Korea), or if people believe the president deceived them (Vietnam, Mexican-American War).

   Pages ....

3. **"The young and better educated college graduates were the ones who showed least support for the war in Vietnam."**

False. These groups gave higher support to the war between 1968 and 1971 than those less educated or older, according to survey research conducted by John E. Mueller in *War, Presidents, and Public Opinion.*

Pages ....

4. **"Economic advantage always determines American foreign policy."**

False. Vietnam investments and trade were insignificant for the American economy, yet the war cost over $200 billion. Support for Israel has been a key part of American Middle East policy, yet it is in the Arab states that oppose Israel that the United States has most of its investments in the region. The United States, until very recently, did not recognize Communist China, in spite of its potential market and trade. Economic calculations form only one factor in American foreign policy making.

Pages ....

DATA CHECK

FIGURES 20.1, 20.2   Trends in Support for the War in Vietnam, by Education and by Age, p. 560

1. The vertical axis in each figure indicates the percentage of respondents supporting administration policy in Vietnam. The horizontal axis indicates the year the polls were taken. Figure 20.1 shows respondents grouped according to educational level. Figure 20.2 shows groupings based on age.

2. Note the upward surge of support from all respondents in the initial phase of the war (1965), followed by various ups and downs (1966), and then a steady decline with fairly small fluctuations. Note the increase in support in 1969, with the advent of a new administration pledged to end the war, until the Cambodian invasion of 1970. This indicates that both Johnson and Nixon initially won support for "new" policies. Was this the "honeymoon" effect?

3. It was the grade-school educated and older people who gave least support to the war, even though the mass demonstrations by antiwar groups consisted disproportionately of youthful and college-educated voters.

4. Use the data in these figures to support or refute the hypothesis that it was the young, college-educated population that formed the major constituency in opposition to presidential war-making in Vietnam.

STATE YOUR CASE

Some people think that the Munich–Pearl Harbor paradigm has outlived its usefulness, and that the major danger to world peace is the unwillingness of nations to resolve disputes by accommodation. They believe that, in constitutional terms, the president should not engage unilaterally in war-making but should consult and collaborate with Congress as a further check on presidential power. Others believe that such procedures would unduly weaken the president, and that he must be free to threaten force, or actually use force, to deter would-be aggressors and avoid repetition of the dangerous appeasement policies that characterized the 1930s. What do you think? Should the president be free of congressional restraints on the use of armed forces in hostilities? (In considering your answer, you might wish to focus on particular situations of interest to you, involving Israel, Lebanon, Taiwan, Japan, Berlin, South Africa, or other nations.)

REVIEW EXERCISE

1. Tariffs and quotas are examples of .... politics.

2. The .... nominates ambassadors, and the
   .... confirms them.

3. The president negotiates treaties, which are consented to by the
   .... through a vote of .... of the members.

4. The Constitution gives Congress the power to .... war.

5. Leadership in making foreign policy is centered in the White House or in
   the .... Department.

6. The committee in the Senate that deals with ratification of treaties and
   consents to the appointment of ambassadors is the ....
   .... Committee.

7. Congress can block the sale of arms if it adopts a ....
   .... within thirty days.

8. When entrepreneurial and interest-group politics shape foreign policy,
   .... is the central political arena.

9. When Reagan became president in 1981, he restored the ....
   world view.

ANSWERS

Glossary Completion

1. isolationism
2. War Powers Resolution
3. containment
4. George F. Kennan
5. appeasement
6. domino

Review Exercise

1. interest group
2. president; Senate
3. Senate; two-thirds
4. declare
5. State
6. Foreign Relations
7. concurrent resolution
8. Congress
9. Munich-Pearl Harbor

21 Military Spending

CHAPTER FOCUS

After reading and reviewing the material in this chapter, you should be able to:

1. Summarize theories of the military-industrial complex, and explain why some people believe that defense politics is an approximation of client politics. Trace the evolution of defense expenditures, and indicate whether they have been increasing or decreasing since 1956.

2. Explain why the 1947 and 1949 Defense Reorganization Acts prevented the merger of services in the Defense Department. Review the present structure of the Department, and explain how it contributes to interservice rivalries. Demonstrate why presidents find it difficult to use the Joint Chiefs of Staff to control defense policy-making.

3. Analyze the key allocative decisions of the defense budget. Indicate factors that make the decisions on the budget incremental. Explain how the congressional role in deciding on weapons systems has changed in recent years.

4. Explain how the condition of the defense industry makes necessary a "follow-on" system in the distribution of contracts. Indicate the extent to which "client" defense politics affects U.S. industry, and compare the performance of defense contractors with similar nondefense companies.

5. Explain why the cost-overrun problem is due primarily to bureaucratic rather than political factors, and describe proposed reforms of the system.

GLOSSARY COMPLETION

1. .... Department created in 1947 from existing War and Navy Departments.

2. .... Committee of senior officers that prepares military plans and advises the secretary of defense, president, and Congress.

3. .... Tendency to distribute government contracts so that a production facility remains intact.

4. .... Practice of commissioning firms to produce competing versions of a weapon and awarding the contract to the firm with the best prototype.

5. .... Forces armed with nuclear weapons designed to inflict unacceptable damage on an aggressor.

6. .... Theory that senior military officers and corporate executives determine American defense policies.

7. .... An inter-service military command designed to make it possible to send American forces on short notice to trouble spots.

COMMON MISCONCEPTIONS

1. **"The Joint Chiefs of Staff commands a unified defense establishment."**
   False. The JCS acts as an advisory committee to the president, and does not command the armed forces. The president and secretary of defense use the JCS only to transmit orders to the various major military commands. The representatives to the JCS function as advocates of their own services rather than planners for a unified strategy, and the services remain to some extent independent of each other and rivals for scarce resources.

   Pages ....

2. **"The percentage of GNP devoted to defense appropriations has been increasing steadily since the 1950s."**
   False. The total amount measured in constant dollars declined steadily

between 1956 and 1980. In 1956, 10 percent of the GNP, and in 1980 about 5 percent of the GNP, were devoted to defense outlays.

Pages ....

3. **"Members of Congress from districts with many defense-related contracts give more support to military requests than do other members of Congress."**
   False. Data about congressional voting indicate that the relationship between voting and defense activity is weak or nonexistent. No systematic evidence exists that congressional voting on national defense issues is determined by the defense-related economic factors in districts. However, it is true that individual members of Congress will engage in various activities to preserve and increase the number of military facilities and defense contracts in their own districts.

   Pages ....

4. **"Defense contracting is the most profitable part of the corporate system."**
   False. The margin of profit on sales of defense firms is no more than that of nondefense firms. The ratio of stock prices to stock earnings is less for defense than for nondefense firms. Firms with the highest volume of government defense business generally earn a smaller profit on capital than those less dependent. The defense industry, therefore, is less profitable, more heavily in debt, and less appealing to stock-market investors than the nondefense firms.

   Pages ....

DATA CHECK

TABLE 21.1   Money Spent on National Defense, p. 580

1. The column "Constant (1972) dollars" is a way of converting actual dollar outlays into the amount a dollar was worth in 1978. Before 1978, current outlays must be "inflated" to find the 1978 equivalent, whereas after 1978 totals must be "deflated." This occurs because dollars in 1978 were worth less than dollars in prior years, and more than dollars in subsequent years.

2. The column "As percentage of GNP" gives the share of total GNP accounted for by defense outlays, and is calculated for any year by dividing defense outlays into total GNP.

3. Note the increase in constant-dollar expenditures between 1950 and 1960,

and subsequent and steady decreases between 1970 and 1980. Note the decrease in outlays as a percentage of GNP between 1955 and 1980.

4. How would you use the data in this table if someone told you that Republican presidents always spend more on defense than Democrats?

STATE YOUR CASE

Some people think we should get politics out of the Defense Department, put the nation's defense in the hands of professional military personnel who would advise the president directly, and eliminate most of the civilian policy makers in the Defense Department. Others believe that for the president to function effectively as commander-in-chief, he needs civilian defense analysts to help in making budget and strategic decisions. What do you think? Is warfare too important to be left to the generals? Should the president rely more heavily on professional military persons for his advice?

REVIEW EXERCISE

1. The conventional view of American defense policy-making is that it is an example of .... politics.

2. The theory of the military-industrial complex is that defense policy-making is actually a case of .... politics.

3. Each member of the .... is also the highest-ranking officer in his own service.

4. Under the Constitution the .... is commander-in-chief of the armed forces.

5. Presidents .... and .... both decided to increase military spending levels in peacetime.

6. During the last ten years each major service has received roughly .... as its share of the defense budget.

7. The great majority of the largest industrial corporations receive less than .... percent of their sales from military contracts.

8. Cost .... occur because a new defense item must be invented before it is built or purchased; therefore, they occur for bureaucratic rather than political reasons.

ANSWERS

Glossary Completion

1. Defense
2. Joint Chiefs of Staff
3. follow-on imperative
4. "fly before you buy"
5. strategic
6. military-industrial complex
7. rapid-deployment force

Review Exercise

1. majoritarian
2. client
3. Joint Chiefs of Staff
4. president
5. Carter and Reagan
6. one-third
7. 5%
8. overruns

PART V

The Nature of American Democracy

22 Who Governs?

CHAPTER FOCUS

After reading and reviewing the material in this chapter, you should be able to:

1. Provide definitions of, and examples for, the four different types of policy outputs of government. You will find it helpful to review Chapters 14–21 on policy-making and the corresponding sections of this Handbook.

2. Explain the function of public opinion in the four types of policy outputs. Under what circumstances is the public most influential? least influential?

3. Describe the Marxist, power elite, bureaucratic, and pluralist theories. Indicate the utilities and shortcomings of each theory as described by the text. You will find it helpful to review the chapters on policy-making and the corresponding sections of this Handbook.

STATE YOUR CASE

There are several competing theories of the distribution of political power in modern society. These were sketched in Chapter 1, and throughout the textbook reference has been made to their utility. The text concludes that "no single description of the entire political system seems adequate." Do you agree? Which of the competing theories do you think best describes the realities of American government?

23 To What Ends?

After reading and reviewing the material in this chapter, you should be able to:

1. Think seriously about the purposes of government and the ends to which political power should be used.

2. Understand how the Framers established constitutional mechanisms that would attempt to reconcile popular government and majority rule with personal freedom and protection of property and civil rights.

3. Summarize the kinds of criticisms made about our political institutions by liberals and conservatives.

4. Theorize about what American policy-making would be like if the United States had adopted a parliamentary system.

5. Describe several of the "idea-based" changes in American politics and contrast these changes with the situation when politics involved merely brokerage of group interests.

STATE YOUR CASE

Several trends in American politics have been noted: greater centralization, greater activism for government in solving social and economic problems; a larger role for interest groups and a decline in party organizations; and increased disenchantment with the performance of governmental officials. With the coming to power of the Reagan administration in 1981, do you think these trends will continue? In the past year what key events have occurred that seem to promise a reversal of these trends? What events seem to indicate a continuation? On balance, do you think major transformations in American politics are occurring, or is it still "politics as usual"?

APPLICATIONS

EXERCISE 1

The Constitutional Dimension

A common misconception among students of American politics is that the national government consists of a set of separate institutions (the president, Congress, and the courts) that exercise distinct powers (executive, legislative, and judicial). But in reality, as your study of Chapters 2, 10, 11, and 13 of the textbook and your work in the Handbook have made clear, the American system of government consists of separate institutions that share and sometimes compete fiercely for powers. The president shares in the legislative power, and Congress shares in the executive power.

A. The Sharing of Powers

You can demonstrate that the Constitution provides for a sharing of power. Turn to the Constitution at the end of your textbook, and consider various provisions of Article I and Article II. Answer the following questions by filling in the blanks:

1. The president of the Senate of the United States is the .... of the United States.

2. When the president of the United States is tried by the Senate in an

impeachment, the presiding officer is the .... of the United States.

3. The times, places, and manner of holding elections for senators and representatives may be determined by the state ....

4. Bills must be passed by the House and ...., and then signed into law by the ....

5. If the .... vetoes a bill passed by the ...., it may become law by a .... vote of each chamber of ....

6. The president, by and with the advice and consent of the ...., makes treaties with foreign nations.

7. The .... nominates ambassadors, but the .... must consent.

8. Justices of the Supreme Court are nominated by the .... with the advice and consent of the ....

9. Officers of the United States are nominated by the .... with the advice and consent of the .... Appointments to inferior offices may be provided for by ....

B. The Competition for Power

Another common misconception is to assume that the Constitution provides a complete blueprint for the working of government. In fact, the document raises as many questions as it answers about the authority of the president and Congress. You can demonstrate that the Constitution is "underdefined," incomplete, ambiguous, and silent at key points by examining in more detail Article II, which deals with presidential power. See if you can find any *specific* words or phrases in Article II that can be used to answer the following constitutional questions:

1. In case of death, resignation, disability, or removal of a president, does the vice-president succeed to the "Office of President," take the oath and become president, or does he exercise only the "powers and duties" of the president, serving as "acting president"?

2. In the event of a double vacancy, does Article II forbid a midterm election to

fill a vacancy in the presidential office? (*Hint:* If the original Constitution were clear on these matters, why was it necessary to pass the Twenty-Fifth Amendment?)

3. Does the president's oath of office require him to faithfully execute every law passed by Congress? Could a president refuse to execute a law in an emergency if he believed that by obeying the law he might be endangering the nation? Must a president obey a law that he believes is a violation of the Constitution?

4. As commander-in-chief, does the president have the constitutional authority to send troops into hostilities in a foreign nation without obtaining a declaration of war from Congress? Is the president given constitutional power to declare American neutrality in a conflict involving other nations, without obtaining concurrence from Congress?

5. May the president unilaterally abrogate a treaty made with a foreign nation, or must he obtain the consent of the Senate?

6. May the president unilaterally recognize a foreign nation? May he withdraw recognition without the consent of the Senate?

7. Where in Article II does the president obtain the authority to negotiate "executive agreements" with other nations without obtaining approval of the Senate or Congress?

8. Where in Article II does the president obtain the power to remove department officials who have been confirmed by the Senate?

9. What constitutional authority permits the president to refuse to spend money appropriated by Congress?

When the president exercises these powers, it is not necessarily the case that he is acting "unconstitutionally." But you should be aware of the fact that the Constitution did not *plainly* state the power or assign it to the president. In each case presidents must do what you tried to do: *interpret* the Constitution so that the power to act could be implied. In fact, it is this process of interpreting the Constitution to expand the powers of the government that is at the heart of the political process.

Now examine Article I of the Constitution. See if you can find any language that Congress might use to imply that it had concurrent power in war-making, treaty-making, diplomatic recognition, executive agreements, and removals from office. See if you can find language in Article I to indicate that Congress has the same powers that the president claims and exercises.

C. The Checks and Balances System

In addition to the two characteristics of the constitutional system that you have already demonstrated—the sharing of powers and the competition for power—there is a third characteristic: the checks and balances system. You can show, simply by reading the Constitution, that any branch may be checked and balanced by one or both of the other branches. Consider Article III, which deals with the judiciary. By examining this article, and any other provisions of the Constitution that deal with the judiciary, you can fill in the blanks to the following questions:

1. The inferior courts of the judiciary of the United States are established by the .... of the United States.

2. In cases other than those involving original jurisdiction mentioned in Article III, Section 2, the Supreme Court shall have appellate jurisdiction, with such exceptions, and under such regulations, as the .... shall make.

3. The trial of all crimes shall be by ....

4. Justices of the Supreme Court are nominated by the ...., with the advice and consent of the ....

Query: There are at present nine justices on the Supreme Court. If the president and Congress were dissatisfied with their opinions, could they "pack" the Court by providing for an additional ten justices, thus providing an instant majority for a different point of view? See if you can find anything in the Constitution that prevents Congress by law from enlarging or contracting the membership of the Supreme Court.

D. Constitutional Interpretation

Everyone, whether public official or private citizen, must decide whether he or she will take a restrictive or expansive view of the language of the Constitution. Consider carefully the views of two Republican presidents, Theodore Roosevelt and William Howard Taft. They were close political allies (Taft was Roosevelt's hand-picked successor), yet they differed sharply in their views of proper constitutional interpretation. In fact, their disagreement was so extreme that it temporarily split the Republican party in 1912, and in a three-sided race both men lost a contest for the White House to the Democrat Woodrow Wilson—himself a great political scientist and scholar.

As you read these selections, consider which view more realistically represents the situation that a modern president must face. But also consider which author seems to have understood the problems involved in abuses of presidential power such as Watergate demonstrated.

Theodore Roosevelt: The "Stewardship" Theory of the Presidency Based on an Expansive Interpretation of the Constitution

The most important factor in getting the right spirit in my Administration, next to the insistence upon courage, honesty, and a genuine democracy of desire to serve the plain people, was my insistence upon the theory that the executive power was limited only by specific restrictions and prohibitions appearing in the Constitution or imposed by the Congress under its constitutional powers.

My view was that every executive officer, and above all every executive officer in high position, was a steward of the people bound actively and affirmatively to do all he could for the people, and not to content himself with the negative merit of keeping his talents undamaged in a napkin. I declined to adopt the view that what was imperatively necessary for the nation could not be done by the President unless he could find some specific authorization to do it. My belief was that it was not only his right but his duty to do anything that the needs of the nation demanded, unless such action was forbidden by the Constitution or by the laws. Under this interpretation of executive power I did and caused to be done many things not previously done by the President and the heads of the departments. I did not usurp power, but I did greatly broaden the use of executive power. In other words, I acted for the public welfare, I acted for the common well-being of all our people, whenever and in whatever manner was necessary, unless prevented by direct constitutional or legislative prohibition. . . .

The course I followed, of regarding the Executive as subject only to the people, and, under the Constitution, bound to serve the people affirmatively in cases where the Constitution does not explicitly forbid him to render the service, was substantially the course followed by both Andrew Jackson and Abraham Lincoln. Other honorable and well-meaning Presidents, such as James Buchanan, took the opposite and, as it seems to me, narrowly legalistic view that the President is the servant of Congress rather than of the people, and can do nothing, no matter how necessary it be to act, unless the Constitution explicitly commands the action. Most able lawyers who are past middle age take this view, and so do large numbers of well-meaning, respectable citizens.

William Howard Taft: The President Must Exercise His Powers Pursuant to the Express or Implied Provisions of the Constitution and the Laws of the Land

The true view of the Executive functions is, as I conceive it, that the President can exercise no power which cannot be fairly and reasonably traced to some specific grant of power or justly implied and included within such express grant as proper and necessary to its exercise. Such specific grant must be either in the federal Constitution or in an act of Congress passed in pursuance thereof. There is no undefined residuum of power which he can exercise because it seems to him to be in the public interest, and there is nothing in the Neagle case and its definition of a law of the United States, or in other precedents, warranting such an inference. The grants of Executive power are necessarily in general terms in order not to embarrass the Executive within the field of action plainly marked for him, but his jurisdiction must be justified and vindicated by affirmative constitutional or statutory provision, or it does not exist.

. . . We have had Presidents who felt the public pulse with accuracy, who played their parts upon the political stage with histrionic genius and commanded the people almost as if they were an army and the President their Commander in Chief. Yet in all these cases, the good sense of the people has ultimately prevailed and no danger has been done to our political structure and the reign of law has continued. In such times when the Executive power seems to be all prevailing, there have always been men in this free and intelligent people of ours, who apparently courting political humiliation and disaster have registered protest against this undue Executive domination and this use of the Executive power and popular support to perpetuate itself.

The Constitution does give the President wide discretion and great power, and it ought to do so. It calls from him activity and energy to see that within his proper sphere he does what his great responsibilities and opportunities require. He is no figurehead, and it is entirely proper that an energetic and active clear-sighted people, who, when they have work to do, wish it done well, should be willing to rely upon their judgment in selecting their Chief Agent, and having selected him, should entrust to him all the power needed to carry out their governmental purpose, great as it may be.

Reprinted from *Our Chief Magistrate and His Powers* (New York: Columbia University Press, 1916), pp. 139, 156–157.

E. The Amendment Process

The Constitution of the United States has been amended twenty-......................... times. For every amendment that has been ratified, there are dozens that have failed to pass Congress or win the approval of three-fourths of the states. At any given time there are many proposals being considered, and one or two amendments in the process of ratification by the states. In the following exercise you will learn how to conduct research on the status of a constitutional amendment.

Our example is the Equal Rights Amendment. It has been introduced in every session of Congress since 1923, yet only in the late 1960s was it taken seriously. On March 22, 1972, it was passed by the necessary two-thirds vote in Congress and sent to state legislatures for ratification. The text of the amendment is as follows:

Section 1. Equality of rights under the law shall not be denied or abridged by the United States or by any state on account of sex.

Section 2. The Congress shall have power to enforce, by appropriate legislation, the provisions of this article.

Section 3. This amendment shall take effect two years after date of ratification.

1. Proposed amendments introduced to Congress are found in the *Digest of Public General Bills and Selected Resolutions*, issued in five cumulative volumes for each session. The best way to find out about congressional action on an amendment that passed Congress is to consult annual volumes of *Congressional Quarterly Almanac*. Use the *Almanac* for 1972 to find out about action taken on the ERA.

2. If you wish to read the speeches made by members of Congress in the debates, consult the *Congressional Record* for the week prior to the March 22, 1972, vote.

3. Proposed constitutional amendments are considered by the two Committees on the Judiciary of Congress. The hearings of these committees are listed in the card catalog under U.S. Congress, Senate, and U.S. Congress, House, by name of the committee. Reports issued by these committees, which summarize the positions of the members, are listed, by name of committee, in the *Monthly Catalog of U.S. Government Publications*, accompanied by a report number. Consult the *Monthly Catalog* for late 1971 or early 1972. When you find a report on ERA listed, obtain the report number and match it against the *Numerical List of Reports and Documents* (which you will obtain from the reference librarian), in order to find the volume in which the report is located in your library.

4. You can determine the positions of the Republicans and Democrats on ERA at their national conventions of 1972, 1976, and 1980 by consulting the *New York Times Index* and then using microfilms of the *New York Times* to read sections of the party platforms that dealt with the amendment.

5. The positions of various presidents on ERA can be determined by using the index to the *Public Papers of the Presidents of the United States* and the *Weekly Compilation of Presidential Documents*. In speeches, news conferences, press releases, or other papers, Presidents Nixon, Ford, Carter, and Reagan took

positions on state ratification of ERA. Does it seem to you that any of these presidents made state ratification a major priority for their administrations?

6. You can find out how the public viewed the amendment by consulting the *Gallup Opinion Index* volumes since 1972.

7. Find out the action your state has taken on ERA by using the *Congressional Quarterly Almanac*. It will provide a listing of states that did not ratify the amendment. By the summer of 1978 not enough states had ratified the ERA to meet the seven-year deadline imposed by Congress. In order to continue the struggle, feminist groups asked Congress to pass a provision extending the time limit for ratification. Use *Congressional Quarterly Almanac* for 1978 to find out the following: what Congress did about the request; which party gave the request the most support; and what the position of President Carter was. You can also determine the actions of your own senators or representative by using the *Congressional Record*.

8. As of summer 1982, five states that had originally ratified the amendment had reversed themselves and rescinded their approval. Consult the provisions of the Constitution that deal with amendments. Do they make any provision for permitting a state to rescind its approval prior to ratification by three-quarters of the states? The Justice Department has said that Congress will have to decide whether or not states have the authority to rescind their original vote. Do you think Congress should have that power? Do you think the issue should be decided by the Supreme Court? Do you think states should have the right to rescind approval of a constitutional amendment?

9. ERA failed to win ratification by the deadline, June 30, 1982. Reintroduced in Congress two weeks later, the whole struggle began all over again!

EXERCISE 2

The Federal System

The national government provides goods and services to people in two ways. It makes payments to states and localities through an intergovernmental grant system, and it makes direct payments to individuals through the transfer systems. Most people never stop to consider just how important both systems are in their lives. By reading Chapter 3 of the textbook, you have become aware of the tremendous growth of both these systems in the past two decades. But most citizens do not realize how reliant they are on the federal government. Consider Tulsa, Oklahoma, a thriving area of the "Sunbelt," proud of its own civic efforts and strongly conservative in its insistence that the role of the federal government be limited. As the following selection indicates, the people of Tulsa and their elected officials are far more tied into the intergovernmental grant system than they think.

U.S. Aid Contradicts Tulsa's Image of Independence

When James I. Inhofe, a young Republican, was inaugurated as Mayor last year, he expressed concern because Tulsa was receiving $21 million a year in Federal aid, a dependence on Washington that runs counter to the city's image of itself as a center of free enterprise and independence.

Reprinted from John Herbers, *The New York Times*, February 2, 1979. © 1979 by The New York Times Company. Reprinted by permission.

However, two economists from the University of Tulsa discovered after extensive research that the amount was not $21 million but more than $48 million in direct Federal grants in 1978. They also found that 27 percent of Tulsa's services of the kind that cities traditionally provide, such as protection of property, community health and environment, transportation and general administration of government, came from Washington.

Although cities vary widely in their structure, what has happened here is typical of many expanding cities and is one example of how, in only a decade, a new form of government has emerged, one so complex and so fragmented that much of it eludes the public view.

•　•　•

The importance of Federal dollars to Tulsa was obscured by the existence of layers of separate trusts or authorities—for urban renewal and other services. These receive Federal money, but their finances are frequently hidden from the public and at times from elected officials.

For example, the Tulsa Urban Renewal Authority receives Federal community development grants through the city, yet reports no financial data in the city budget.

•　•　•

If all the Federal money that comes to Tulsa, to both groups and individuals, were added up, the total would be $450 million a year, or 22 times the Mayor's estimate, according to one Federal study.

Tulsa now has an estimated population of 356,000 and is dominant in a metropolitan area of 528,000 people that prospers in part because it has been opened to barge traffic in the Gulf of Mexico by a large public works project pushed through Congress by Oklahoma's senators and representatives.

•　•　•

There is a new City Hall and Convention Center Complex, where the annual international rodeo finals were held this week, a pedestrian mall on main street, a performing arts center that is home for Tulsa's opera and ballet companies, and a hotel and shopping center with an ice skating rink.

About $158 million has been spent on redevelopment, with $100 million of this coming from private investment and the rest from Federal and city funds.

But Tulsans are not often reminded of the Federal role, and Mayor Inhofe said that he was preparing for future cuts in Federal grants. However, the city would not be hurt by the budget cuts proposed by President Carter because it is not deeply involved in the programs that face cuts.

A. Is the Federal System Becoming More Centralized?

Some people believe that the national government's increasing scope and level of activities are seriously imbalancing the federal system. They claim that the responsibility of state and local governments to provide goods and services is

---

TABLE 2.1 State Revenues and Expenditures, Federal Receipts and Outlays (billions of dollars)

Year	State		Federal	
	Revenues	Expenditures	Receipts	Outlays
1972	$112.3	$109.2	$208.6	$232.0
1974	140.7	132.1	264.9	269.6
1976	185.2	181.9	300.0	366.5
1978	225.0	203.8	402.0	450.8

Sources: Data for this and the following tables from U.S. Bureau of the Census, *State Government Finance, 1977,* and *Statistical Abstract of the U.S., 1977.*

decreasing, and call for a cutback in the activities and expenditures of the national government to restore the balance. Others believe that when the national government takes an interest in an activity, like building highways or schools, it is likely that the role of state and local governments will increase through a system of intergovernmental cooperation. You can test the hypothesis that the federal system is becoming much more centralized, in favor of the national government, by examining the data in Table 2.1. You may want to find data for later years to complete these tables, under the supervision of your instructor and with the assistance of the reference librarian.

Which is rising more rapidly, state expenditures or federal outlays? State revenues or federal receipts? State debt or national debt? Do the figures in Tables 2.1 and 2.2 indicate to you that the national percentage of total expenditures of all levels of government has been rising?

TABLE 2.2 State and National Debts (billions of dollars)

Year	State and Local Debt	National Debt
1970	$144	$382.6
1974	206	486.2
1976	240	631.9
1977	259	709.1
1978	280	780.4

TABLE 2.3 Governmental Employment and Payroll, 1950–79

	1950	1955	1960	1965	1970	1975	1979
Federal Civilian	2,117	2,378	2,421	2,558	2,881	2,890	2,869
State	1,057	1,250	1,527	2,028	2,755	3,271	2,699
Local	3,228	3,804	4,860	5,973	7,392	8,813	9,403

Federal government civilian employment has grown by less than one-third since 1950. But note the changes in state employment in the last two decades, and the dramatic growth in local government employment. If, as conservatives argue, state and local government is more responsive to public demands, what would that seem to indicate about the desire of the American public in the last thirty years for more governmental services?

You can compare the information in Tables 2.4 and 2.5 with the materials presented in Chaper 3 of your textbook and the corresponding chapter in this Handbook, which should enable you to write a brief essay on the question: Is the American federal system becoming imbalanced in favor of the national government? Remember, however, that expenditures are only one measure of centralization. Laws or court orders may shift power and responsibility without necessarily changing the levels of expenditure.

TABLE 2.4 National Government Expenditures as Percentage of All Government Expenditures

Year	Percentage
1950	60.3%
1955	63.5
1960	59.7
1965	57.9
1970	55.5
1975	52.3
1978	53.7

TABLE 2.5 **Expenditures by the Federal Government in the Intergovernmental Grant and Transfer Systems (billions of dollars)**

Year	Aid to State and Local Governments	Domestic Transfer Payments
1970	$24.0	$ 54.8
1972	34.1	75.7
1974	43.3	101.7
1976	59.0	153.6
1977	68.3	167.7
1978	77.8	182.0
1979	82.8	201.7

Which of the following do you think is correct? When the national government increases its domestic expenditures, then state expenditures and employment increase. Or, when the national government increases its domestic expenditures, state expenditures and employment decrease.

B. How Domestic Transfer Payments Affect You

As a college student you are affected by many programs of the national government. Federal funds build libraries, laboratories, and dormitories, upgrade facilities for energy conservation and the handicapped, provide part-time employment for scholarship students and fellowships and research funds for faculty. Several federal programs provide grants and loans to meet tuition expenses. Under the Middle Income Assistance Act passed by Congress on November 1, 1978, federally Guaranteed Student Loans (GSL) are available to all students, regardless of financial status. Basic Education Opportunity Grant (BEOG) funds are available now to students whose family income is less than $25,000, and the maximum payment has been raised to $1,800.

Whether or not such programs provide adequate benefit levels depends partly on requests that a president makes to Congress in his budget, partly on actions Congress takes in appropriating funds, and partly on the way programs are administered. In short, whether or not you are eligible for a grant, whether or not you receive one, and whether or not you receive as much as you need—all these issues are resolved in a *political* process.

For example, both Presidents Carter and Reagan, in their budget requests to

Congress, proposed severe cutbacks in student scholarship and loan programs from levels Congress had funded in the 1970s. Congress had provided for loans at low interest rates with eligibility ceilings. Without any changes, these programs in 1981–82 would have cost an estimated $3.2 billion. With cuts made by Congress the program cost $2.8 billion.

Because of these cuts, approximately one-third of the three million student borrowers became ineligible for loans under the new rules. Congress also cut a program that gave grants to low-income students. Maximum grants were cut from $1,750 to $1,670 a year, and a revised eligibility scale eliminated more than 250,000 students from the program, mostly those whose family income ranged from $16,000 to $25,000.

The cuts in the guaranteed student loan program hit particularly hard at middle-income families whose children attended public universities, but left almost untouched the families with higher incomes whose children attended more expensive private universities. The following are some of the changes instituted in 1981:

- an origination fee of 5 percent on all loans.
- restoration of an eligibility test based on family income (which had been eliminated in 1978). Students are automatically eligible if their families' adjusted incomes are below $30,000.
- students from families with larger incomes may be eligible if they can demonstrate need. This will eliminate most students attending public colleges with low or moderate tuition if family income is between $45,000 and $30,000. It will permit students attending expensive private colleges to borrow funds unless family income is above $54,000 (if there is one child attending college) or $110,000 (if two children attend).

The budget proposals presented to Congress by the Reagan administration in February, 1982, had the following provisions:

- funding for Pell Grants at $1.4 billion.
- elimination of graduate students from the Guaranteed Student Loan program.
- increase in the origination fee for the GSL program from 5 percent to 10 percent.
- elimination of the Supplemental Educational Opportunity Grant program and the State Student Incentive Grant program, both of which were targeted at lower-income students.
- elimination of federal funding for the National Direct Student Loan program (loans would be made only from the existing university funds).
- cuts in the work-study program funding of 20 percent.
- a four-year phaseout of the Social Security funding of students from families in which the working parent is disabled or deceased.

You can use *Congressional Quarterly Almanac*s for 1982 and 1983 to see what happened to student-aid programs and determine which party took responsibility for the new policies.

To find out how the activities of Congress, the president, and the Office of Education of the Department of Health, Education, and Welfare affect you, you can check several sources of information. It is very easy to find out what is happening. Simply ask the financial aid office of your college for the following: Office of Education *BSFA Newsletter*, the National Association of Student Financial Aid Administrators *Newsletter*, and the American Council on Education *Higher Education and National Affairs*. Each of these bulletins informs you of what to expect. (The best months to examine are January and February, when the issues of these periodicals review the presidential budget proposals and their impact should Congress adopt them.)

You might find it interesting to use these sources to write a short term paper on the impact of federal funding on the financial aid program of your college. By comparing the amount of federal aid received by your school in 1961, 1971, and 1981, you will obtain an understanding of the impact of federal grant and transfer payments on the higher-education establishment.

EXERCISE 3

Surveying the Political Culture

Political scientists and pollsters use surveys of public opinion to determine what people think about politics. While you and your classmates do not have the time or resources to conduct a national survey, you can use your knowledge of the political culture, gained in Chapter 4, to conduct a survey of your own class to determine the attitudes of students on your campus. Review the concepts presented in your textbook before attempting to measure some of the following dimensions.

(1) Cynicism and mistrust of governmental officials and institutions.
(2) The sense of personal efficacy and competence in being able to influence government.
(3) The responsibility to participate in political affairs.
(4) The proportion of conservative, moderate, and liberal students.

When you have conducted these surveys, you can compare your findings with some of the data presented in the textbook. Do you find that your classmates are highly politicized, or are they mostly cynical about politics and hesitant to participate? Do you find your classmates eager to exercise their right to vote, or are they like so many people aged 18–25, who have the lowest voting rate of any age group? Are most students in your class moderates or liberals, as most students were in the 1960s, or has there been a definite "swing to the right" as the conservatives have claimed?

You can also compare your findings with poll data reported by the Louis Harris and George Gallup organizations. Periodically, local newspapers publish the findings of these organizations, involving questions very similar to the ones presented here.

Note: Your survey of student attitudes cannot be used to generalize about students all over America. Only a carefully drawn sample of students with geographic, racial, ethnic, religious, and socioeconomic diversity can be used to make generalizations.

Test 1. Cynicism and Mistrust of Government

	Agree	Disagree
1. Most politicians look out for their constituents more than for themselves.	....	....
2. The major parties are run by the rich for their own interests.	....	....
3. Most politicians can't be bribed.	....	....
4. Most politicians are controlled by groups not known to the public.	....	....
5. No matter what anyone thinks, a few people always run things.	....	....
6. Most politicians don't mean what they say.	....	....
7. There is little connection between what politicians say and what they do once they are elected.	....	....
8. All politicians are controlled by the bosses.	....	....
9. I have a great deal of confidence that the government will do what is right.	....	....
10. Politicians place their own interests above the interests of the public.	....	....

Test 2. Feelings of Competence and Efficacy

	Agree	Disagree
1. Public officials don't care much about what people like me think.	....	....
2. The way people vote is the main thing that decides how things are run in this country.	....	....
3. Voting is the only way that people like me can have a say about how government acts.	....	....
4. People like me have little say about what the government does.	....	....
5. Our community could get together to change an unjust law if we wished to do so.	....	....

Test 3. Feelings of Political Obligation

	Agree	Disagree
1. It isn't so important to vote if your party doesn't have a chance to win.	....	....
2. Many local elections aren't important enough to bother with.	....	....
3. So many people vote in national elections that it doesn't matter if I vote or not.	....	....
4. To be a good citizen one need only be honest and fair in personal matters; one needn't participate in politics.	....	....

Test 4. Liberal and Conservative Attitudes

	Agree	Disagree
1. Senior citizens should be given adequate pensions, even if their social security contributions have been inadequate.	....	....
2. The government should finance college for all qualified students in need.	....	....
3. The government should create jobs for those people who are unemployed.	....	....
4. Government should regulate business more than it should regulate labor.	....	....
5. It is more important to spend money on social welfare programs than to balance the national budget.	....	....
6. It is more important to spend money on social problems than to enact a tax cut.	....	....
7. It is more important to deal with unemployment than to deal with inflation.	....	....
8. Government-owned utilities are effective and beneficial to the public.	....	....
9. The national government should provide food stamps to people who cannot pay the market price for food.	....	....
10. The national government has an obligation to provide rent subsidies to those who cannot pay rents set by landlords.	....	....

EXERCISE 4
Elections and Voting Participation

In a democracy the participation of a mass electorate is essential, not only to determine the outcome of contests for public office, but also to provide legitimacy for the political system. It is not enough simply to be personally honest and good in social and economic dealings to be a good citizen—one must also participate in the political life of the nation.

Yet in the 1960s and 1970s, voting rates declined. More and more people were voting in successive elections, but a smaller percentage of those eligible to vote were participating. At the same time, other forms of participation were increasing, such as working for a candidate, giving money, or electioneering. One could either take the pessimistic view—that the future of democracy was in question when so many people were "dropping out"—or the optimistic view—that, for those who remained, the system was more open, more accessible, and more responsive than ever before.

The activities in this section are designed to acquaint you with some of the research methods used by political scientists to study problems of political participation.

A. Measuring Political Activity

Various surveys have been used by political scientists to delineate trends involving various forms of activity. You can conduct such a poll to determine the level of participation among students in your school. Use the following questions.

In the last four years, have you engaged in any of the following activities on behalf of a political party or a candidate for public office?

	Yes	No
Belonged to a party club?	....	....
Worked for a political party?	....	....
Attended a party meeting?	....	....
Given money to a party?	....	....
Given money to a candidate?	....	....
Attended a gathering at which a candidate spoke?	....	....
Worn a button or displayed a bumper sticker?	....	....
Given your opinion to others about a party or candidate?	....	....
Followed an election campaign in the newspapers?	....	....
Followed an election campaign on radio?	....	....
Followed an election campaign on television?	....	....

You should find an interesting result: the highest forms of "participation" are those in which candidates are communicating their messages to citizens, and the lowest forms of participation are those in which citizens attend party meetings and work for political clubs. Most people, in other words, are passive consumers of political communication directed to them, and are not active producers of political activity directed toward others.

B. Rates of Participation in Elections

The Committee for the Study of the American Electorate found that in 1980 the turnout in presidential elections declined to its lowest point in almost half a century, and the turnout in the off-year election, 1978, was the lowest since 1942. When slightly more than 50 percent of the eligible electorate votes in a presidential election, and the winning candidate receives slightly more than half of that vote, it means that only 25 percent of the American electorate has backed the winning candidate. When only 39 percent of the electorate votes for congressional candidates in an off-year election, even if the winners get two-thirds of the votes in each contest, it still means that only 26 percent of the American electorate has backed the winning members of Congress. Voter apathy in the states of New York, New Jersey, and Connecticut is so acute that the governors of these states in the late 1970s each won elections with the votes of less than 25 percent of the eligible electorate.

Several reasons have been offered to explain the low and declining voting rates. The *sociological* reason is that members of minority groups, and low-income groups, feel "disconnected" from the political system, do not believe that voting is of any use to them, do not think the system will respond to their needs, and therefore they do not vote. The *institutional* reason is that cumbersome registration procedures discourage people from registering, and without registering they cannot vote in the general election. The *psychological* reason is that, in the words of pollster Louis Harris, "Voters feel like losers," and that levels of alienation, powerlessness, and disenchantment with politicians have increased dramatically in the 1960s and 1970s.

Without trying to untangle the various possible reasons why people don't vote (something that even professional political scientists have been unable to accomplish), it is possible for you to conduct a brief and simple exercise that will demonstrate to you how serious this problem of nonparticipation really is.

1. First, obtain the *County and City Data Book, 1980* or *America Votes, 1980* (Volume 13). You will find listed the population of your county from the 1970 census. To make a rough calculation of the number of eligible voters, multiply the population by .70 on a calculator. The result will be the voting-age population, or VAP. Thus, if the population of your county were listed as 400,000, you would multiply that number by .70 to obtain a VAP of 280,000.

   Next, add up the total number of people who voted for president in your county in 1980. Make sure you add all the totals for all candidates, not just for President Reagan. Divide the number of voters you have obtained by the VAP, and you will obtain the *turnout rate*.

   Note: The most common mistake that students make at this point is to divide the VAP by the number of voters. This generally yields a number between 1 and 2. To perform the operation correctly, always remember that the VAP will be larger than the number who voted, since more people are eligible to vote than actually did vote, and therefore the *larger number* always goes into the *smaller number* when you do the division to obtain the turnout rate.

   Thus, if the VAP in your county were 280,000, and if 140,000 people voted for president in 1976, you would divide 140,000 by 280,000, resulting in a turnout rate of 50 percent. (You would have made a mistake if you divided 280,000 by 140,000, because then the number on your calculator would be 2, an obvious error.)

2. Using Michael Barone *et al.*, *The Almanac of American Politics*, choose the two counties in your state with the highest median incomes, and perform the same calculations. Do you find that most people in the richest counties vote for president? Or do you find that even in the richest counties a substantial proportion of the population does not vote for president? What do you find for the two counties with the lowest median incomes?

3. Refer again to *The Almanac of American Politics*. Find the population of your congressional district, multiply by .70 to obtain the VAP, and then divide by the number of voters in the congressional elections of 1978 and 1980 to obtain the turnout rates for presidential years and off-years. Consult the *Congressional District Data Book* for the number of voters in congressional elections.

Are turnout rates higher in midterm or presidential election years? Did more people vote for president or for a member of Congress in your district in 1980? Does a majority of the VAP turn out to vote in congressional races in either election year?

Compare the most affluent congressional district in your state with the least affluent. Are there significant differences in turnout rates?

4. Consult *America Votes, 1980* (Volume 13). Turn to the section on New York State, New York City. You will find the city of New York divided into various *assembly districts*, with the vote for president listed for each district. Compare the most affluent district of the city, the East Side of Manhattan, with one of the least affluent districts in the South Bronx. Each of these districts has approximately the same population, and therefore approximately the same VAP. Note the high turnout on the East Side of Manhattan and the incredibly low rates in the South Bronx. Consult *The Almanac of American Politics* on New York City *congressional districts*. Why are there districts in the city in which a member can be elected to Congress with less than 20 percent of the VAP participating? Can you find anything in the descriptions of these congressional districts that might offer clues to the low rates of participation?

C. Presidential Coattails

One of the recurring myths of American politics is that the president has "coattails," on which members of his party who are running for lower offices may ride to victory by identifying with him. In fact, candidates for Congress and the Senate from the president's party usually receive a larger margin of the two-party vote than the president does. You can use Barone's *Almanac of American Politics* to demonstrate to yourself that in most states Carter in 1976 received a smaller margin of the two-party vote than did the victorious Senate and House candidates of the Democratic party.

But in most elections the presidential candidate will "lead the ticket," that is, he will receive more total votes than anyone else from his party in the state. This is true because, even if his margin of victory is lower, more people vote for the presidency than for other offices. Thus, if Carter and Ford each got one million votes in a state, and Carter got 50 percent of the two-party vote, he would still "lead the ticket," if in the Senate race the Democratic candidate received 900,000 votes, and the Republican candidate received 600,000 votes (even though the Democrats' margin of victory was 60 percent).

Did President Carter "lead the ticket" in total votes in 1976?

1. Use the *Almanac* to determine which states conducted Senate races in 1976. Then add up the total votes for Democratic Senate candidates from these states. Now add up the total vote for Carter from these same states. Did Carter obtain more total votes in his race than Democratic Senate candidates obtained in theirs? Were there states in which Carter did *not* "lead the ticket"?

2. Examine the election results in your state, using Barone, *Almanac of American Politics*, and *America Votes, 1976*, Volume 12. In the 1976 presidential elections, which contest had the highest turnout of voters? Which candidate, for what office, received the most votes? In which races were the margins of victory the highest? In which contests were the races the most competitive? Did Carter achieve such a dramatic success in your state that it could be claimed that his coattails brought other Democrats their victories?

3. Use *America Votes, 1972* to examine the effect of Nixon's election victory on the fortunes of the Republican candidates for the U.S. Senate. Compare Nixon's margins of victory and vote totals with those of Republican Senate candidates. Could you argue that Nixon had coattails?

4. In 1976 there seemed to be some correlation between Democratic control of the state legislatures and Carter's electoral success. In the twenty-one states in which Democrats controlled the lower house by a better than 70 percent margin in seats, Carter won eighteen. In fourteen states in which the Democrats controlled the lower house by a margin of 60 to 70 percent, Carter won only five. And Carter won only one state in which the Democratic margin was less than 60 percent and in which Republicans controlled the lower chamber.

    Table 4.1 indicates the percentage of seats that Republicans held in the lower house of the state legislatures after the 1980 elections. It might interest you to construct a correlation graph to see if there is any connection between Republican strength at the legislative level and the Reagan victory in the presidential elections. If a close correlation existed, then one could argue either that Reagan benefited from the strength of state legislative parties, or alternatively, that Reagan's coattails helped these parties.

    a. How did Reagan do in states in which Republicans control the lower house?

    b. How did Reagan do in states where Republicans have at least 40 percent of the seats in the lower house?

    c. How did Reagan do in states in which Republicans have less than 40 percent of the seats in the lower house?

5. Repeat step 1 using Republican Senate races in 1980 to determine if President Reagan led the ticket.

TABLE 4.1   Control of State Lower-House Seats and Electoral College Success, 1980

State	Republican Seats	State	Republican Seats
Alabama	3.8%	Montana	56
Alaska	40	Nebraska	(nonpartisan, unicameral)
Arizona	71.6	Nevada	35
Arkansas	7	New Hampshire	60
California	41.2	New Jersey	45
Colorado	60	New Mexico	42
Connecticut	43.7	New York	42.6
Delaware	60.9	North Carolina	20
Florida	32.5	North Dakota	74
Georgia	12.7	Ohio	43.4
Idaho	80	Oklahoma	27.7
Illinois	51.4	Oregon	54
Indiana	63	Pennsylvania	50.7
Iowa	58	Rhode Island	16
Kansas	57.6	South Dakota	70
Kentucky	25	Tennessee	39.4
Louisiana	9.5	Texas	24
Maine	44.4	Utah	76
Maryland	11.3	Vermont	55.3
Massachusetts	20.1	Virginia	25
Michigan	41.8	Washington	57.1
Minnesota	47.7	West Virginia	21
Mississippi	3	Wisconsin	40.4
Missouri	32	Wyoming	62.9

Repeat step 2 to determine if President Reagan had "coattails" in your state in 1980, using *America Votes, 1980,* Volume 13.

D. Popular Votes vs. Electoral Votes

Because of the mechanics of the Electoral College, several presidents have been elected with fewer popular votes than their opponents. In 1824 Andrew Jackson won a plurality of votes but lost to John Quincy Adams after the Electoral

College failed to produce a winner and the contingency election went to the House. In 1876 Rutherford B. Hayes was elected with a minority of the popular vote, as was Benjamin Harrison in 1888.

Most students assume that these examples are merely "history" and that nothing of the sort can happen today. Here is an exercise you can perform to indicate just how "modern" a problem this is. Consider the results of the Kennedy–Nixon contest of 1960. Most results are printed as follows:

	Popular Vote	Electoral Vote
John F. Kennedy (D)	34,220,984	303
Richard M. Nixon (R)	34,108,157	219
Unpledged slates	638,822	15

However, these results may be stated somewhat differently. Alabama votes were counted twice, one time for Kennedy, and one time for unpledged slates of electors. In Alabama in 1960 five electoral votes went to Kennedy, and six went to the unpledged slate in the Electoral College. An alternate computation gives 5/11s of Alabama's Democratic votes to Kennedy and 6/11s to the unpledged slate. Then the more accurate results are:

	Popular Vote	Electoral Vote
John F. Kennedy (D)	34,049,976	303
Richard M. Nixon (R)	34,108,157	219
Unpledged slates	491,547	15

If only five states had shifted from Kennedy to Nixon, which could have occurred if only 0.157 percent of the voters in those states had shifted their vote, Nixon would have been elected president. In 1948 if only three states had shifted from Truman to Dewey, which could have occurred if only 0.275 percent of the voters had shifted, Dewey would have become president.

In the following exercise, consider just how close the election of 1976 was for Carter. Table 4.2 shows the unofficial election returns available at the time the Electoral College met in 1977, as reported in the *Congressional Quarterly Almanac, 1976*. Your goal in this exercise is to shift states from Carter to the Ford column so that:

    a. a minimum number of shifts will produce an Electoral College majority for Ford;

    b. a minimum shift in the popular vote will be necessary to give the election to Ford.

Hint: You should be able to shift fewer than 4,000 votes from the Carter column to the Ford column in each of two states in order to accomplish a change in the election result. Can you find the two states?

If fewer than 8,000 votes are shifted to change the election result, what percentage of the entire electorate was shifted? Compare with the 1948 results and 1960 results.

TABLE 4.2   1976 Presidential Election Results (270 electoral votes needed to win)

State	Popular Vote Carter	Popular Vote Ford	Electoral Vote Carter	Electoral Vote Ford	Percentage Carter	Percentage Ford
Alabama	644,579	495,318	9		56%	43%
Alaska	31,788	55,783		3	36	64
Arizona	294,668	417,413		6	40	57
Arkansas	495,909	266,713	6		65	35
California	3,709,715	3,837,202		45	49	50
Colorado	446,807	566,870		7	43	55
Connecticut	641,010	712,414		8	47	52
Delaware	122,610	109,926	3		52	47
District of Columbia	127,562	25,184	3		84	16
Florida	1,561,383	1,375,296	17		53	46
Georgia	959,663	472,610	12		67	33
Hawaii	147,375	140,003	4		51	49
Idaho	126,362	204,188		4	37	61
Illinois	2,229,605	2,333,260		26	48	51
Indiana	1,006,636	1,169,144		13	46	54
Iowa	619,710	632,486		8	49	50
Kansas	429,008	501,759		7	45	53
Kentucky	612,421	527,956	9		53	47
Louisiana	683,512	606,204	10		52	46
Maine	231,283	234,434		4	49	49
Maryland	735,618	648,980	10		53	47
Massachusetts	1,425,476	1,027,883	14		56	41
Michigan	1,694,388	1,884,867		21	46	53
Minnesota	1,067,894	818,120	10		56	42
Mississippi	373,917	362,056	7		50	49
Missouri	986,185	918,620	12		51	48
Montana	146,696	170,156		4	46	54
Nebraska	230,152	349,736		5	39	59
Nevada	92,088	100,926		3	47	53
New Hampshire	147,618	185,472		4	43	56
New Jersey	1,420,668	1,477,858		17	49	50
New Mexico	199,225	207,718		4	49	51
New York	3,336,665	3,060,695	41		52	48
North Carolina	923,533	738,545	13		56	44
North Dakota	134,503	151,515		3	47	52
Ohio	2,000,035	1,992,460	25		50	49
Oklahoma	530,242	543,221		8	48	51
Oregon	484,643	485,305		6	48	48
Pennsylvania	2,315,494	2,187,038	27		50	49
Rhode Island	216,991	172,138	4		56	44
South Carolina	443,901	342,409	8		56	44
South Dakota	146,153	151,619		4	49	51
Tennessee	822,250	633,228	10		56	43
Texas	2,036,484	1,880,581	26		52	48
Utah	180,974	335,144		4	35	64
Vermont	77,819	99,043		3	43	55
Virginia	810,697	834,605		12	49	51
Washington	643,333	679,631		9	47	51
West Virginia	430,404	311,012	6		58	42
Wisconsin	1,037,056	1,003,039	11		50	48
Wyoming	62,267	92,831		3	40	60
TOTALS	40,274,975	38,530,614	297	241	51%	48%

Source: *Congressional Quarterly Almanac*, 1976, p. 822. Reprinted by permission.

EXERCISE 5

The Media

The mass media (television, radio, newspapers) provide most Americans with the information they use to participate in politics. Politicians use the media to disseminate their point of view, to campaign for votes and for support once in office, and to criticize their opponents' positions. The media do not act as a sounding board however. Legions of investigative reporters constantly attempt to expose wrongdoing, conflict of interest, corruption, and mismanagement. Columnists and editorial writers offer their opinions on the important current events. The media have been called the "fourth branch" of government, and if that be true, then they have potential for wrongdoing, conflict of interest, and misuse of power—just like the formal branches. They also have the potential to influence the opinions of Americans through columnists and editorial writers who defend or criticize official policy.

Political scientists study several different issues involving the media and the government. They are interested in the scope of communication: who reads or listens and who "tunes out" and becomes uninformed and apathetic. The size of the audience may indicate in a general way the "health" of the system, for if no one is listening to what those who govern are saying, then obviously there will be problems. In the late 1970s less than half the television audience tuned into the evening newscasts, a problem of some concern for political science researchers. They are also interested in the content of different media. For example, to what extent does television news provide adequate amounts of information, so that citizens can make informed judgments about events? And finally, they are interested in the *tone* of the media. Are critics who charge that the media are distorted by an "eastern liberal" bias correct? Or are critics who claim that the media are conservative apologists for the administration in power more accurate? In the following three activities, we shall see how political scientists conduct their research to shed some light on these questions.

A. The Dissemination of Information

Political scientists are interested in learning how information is disseminated through the political system. They want to know where people obtain their ideas about politics. You can conduct a survey of students that will provide you with information about the dissemination of political information.

Sources of Information

1. Do you follow public affairs through any of the following sources?

   daily newspaper
   weekly magazine
   radio news
   television news

2. Which do you get the most information from?

   daily newspaper
   weekly magazine
   radio news
   television news
   newspaper and radio
   newspaper and television
   radio and television
   magazine and radio
   magazine and television

3. Which single source do you get the most information from?

   daily newspaper
   weekly magazine
   radio news
   television news

You will be interested to know that, according to the other surveys, a majority of the public obtain their information primarily from television news. Of course, on a college campus, it is conceivable that students will rely more on other sources, especially if access to a private television set is limited.

B. Which Sources of Information Are the Best?

How much information can the public obtain from television news? Is it comparable to what can be obtained by reading a daily newspaper? The following exercise might help you make up your own mind about adequate sources for keeping informed about public affairs.

1. Choose a network station (either ABC, CBS, or NBC), and be prepared to watch the local news and the national news with a tape recorder. Arrange with your library to obtain a copy of a good major newspaper, such as the *New York Times*, the *Washington Post*, the *Philadelphia Inquirer*, the *Los Angeles Times*, or the *Atlanta Constitution*. Also arrange to obtain copies of a local newspaper.

2. For three days watch the news programs on television. Tape record any story dealing with foreign affairs. After three days, determine:
   a. How many stories on foreign affairs were broadcast by the national news? How many stories were broadcast by the local news?
   b. How many minutes did each story run? What was the average length of a foreign affairs story on national news? On local news? (You will rerun the tape, using a watch, to compute the time of each story.)
   c. How many words are contained in the average story broadcast on national news? On local news? You can compute this by determining the approximate words per minute in a story (by running the tape recorder for a minute and counting the words).

3. Examine the major newspaper and the local newspaper coverage of the same stories for the same time period. Determine which stories in the newspapers dealt with the stories broadcast by the news programs.
   a. Using a ruler, determine the number of column inches devoted to each story.
   b. Count the number of words in each column inch, then multiply the number of inches to determine the number of words in each story.
   c. How many words are contained in the average story printed by the major newspaper? How many words are contained in the average story printed by the local newspaper?
   d. List all the foreign affairs stories covered by the national news program for the three-day period. List all the foreign affairs stories covered by the major newspaper for the three-day period. Which source covered more stories? Was there a significant difference?

4. You can construct a table to summarize your results.

	National News Show	Local News Show	National Press	Local Press
Number of stories covered				
Number of words in average story				

You may wish to substitute economic news, presidential news, or any other political topic instead of concentrating on foreign affairs news.

C. Are the Media Critics or Apologists for the System?

Political scientists are also interested in determining the *content* of news stories, to see if their *tone* is supportive of the political system. How do editorial writers and columnists portray political institutions and leaders?

By performing the following exercise, you can learn how to perform a *content analysis* on media portrayal of the presidency. You can then use the material on the "textbook" presidency that appears in Exercise 7 of this Handbook to compare press treatment of the presidency with traditional textbook treatment.

1. Arrange to obtain copies of a major newspaper for six days. If you cannot do so, obtain the *New York Times* on microfilm for a six-day period.

2. Examine any editorials or signed columns of opinion on the inside pages that make mention of the president.

3. Upon reading each article, place a small "X" in each question of the table below. Place the "X" under the "5" column if the article was favorable to the president, and place it under the "1" column if the article was unfavorable. For anything in between, use the other columns.

Dimension	Most Negative 1	2	Neutral 3	4	Most Favorable 5
Expertise of the administration					
Timeliness of the decision					
Success of the policy					
Honesty of subordinates					
Responsiveness to the public					
Secretiveness of officials					

4. Are most of the "Xs" clustered on the negative side of the table? Do you think it is a fair assessment of editorial writers and columnists to state that they view themselves in an adversary relationship with the White House? That they see themselves as perennial critics of the performance of the president? Or do you think the newspapers are primarily apologists for the administration in power?

EXERCISE 6

The Congressional Power Structure

One of the key tenets of democratic theory is that vigorous competition between political parties for public office will produce adequate accountability of the rulers to the ruled. You have learned from reading your textbook Chapter 6 on political parties and Chapter 10 on Congress that such competition does not always exist in practice.

Today a majority of the members of Congress do not face serious competition in party primaries or in general elections. Some political scientists have argued that the legislature has become a career for professional politicians, who are likely to serve twenty years or more in that institution. Samuel Huntington has noted that, whereas in 1900 only 9 percent of the members of the House had served five terms or more, and less than 1 percent had served ten terms, by 1957, 45 percent had served five terms or more, and 14 percent ten terms or more. And by 1970 about one-fifth of the House had served for ten terms or more.

But in the 1970s other political scientists challenged the "careerism" theory and pointed to an increase in turnover in Congress. By 1976, for example, over one-third of the House members were beginning either their first or second terms, and there was substantial turnover due to retirements in 1978, and to defeats and retirements in 1980.

A. Examining Turnover in the House of Representatives and Senate

Table 6.1 presents data on the amount of turnover in the House. Using *Congressional Quarterly Weekly Reports* in November of every even-numbered year after 1976, you can update this table.

TABLE 6.1 House Turnover

| Year | Total | Representatives Seeking Reelection | | Representatives Reelected | |
		Lost Primary	Lost Election	% running	% of House
1966	407	5	40	89	83
1968	404	3	5	98	91
1970	398	8	12	95	87
1972	381	7	13	95	83
1974	391	8	40	88	79
1976	384	3	13	96	85
1978					
1980					
1982					

Which accounts for more turnover in the House—members declining to run for reelection, therefore making way for newcomers, or members defeated in primaries or in the general election? Can Congress still be considered a career for those members who choose to run for reelection?

Consider the data in Table 6.2. Using *Congressional Quarterly Weekly Reports* in November of every even-numbered year after 1976, you can update this table.

TABLE 6.2 Senate Turnover

| Year | Total | Senators Seeking Reelection | | Senators Reelected | | New Senators |
		Lost Primary	Lost Election	%running	#reelected	
1966	32	3	1	88	27	7
1968	28	4	4	71	20	14
1970	30	1	6	77	23	11
1972	27	2	5	71	20	13
1974	27	2	2	85	23	11
1976	25	0	9	64	16	18
1978						
1980						
1982						

Remember that in each election year only 33 or 34 Senate seats are contested. Do you think that the "career" theory of Congress applies fully to the Senate?

List the advantages of careerism in Congress as you see them. What are the disadvantages of careerism for the American political system?

B. The Seniority System

Some congressional delegations have more "seniority" (i.e., terms of service in the chamber) than other delegations. A state that has many members who have served for many terms will gain advantages that come from better committee assignments, more power on committees (i.e., more chairmanships), and a better familiarity with the rules, procedures, and customs of the chamber. Cohesive state delegations with seniority, such as the North Carolinians in the 1960s and the Texans in the 1970s, have wielded power far beyond their numerical strength.

You can find out which states have the advantage of seniority. *The Congressional Directory*, published annually, lists the members of Congress by terms of service. Table 6.3 was prepared for this Handbook to show which states have the advantage of seniority in the House of Representatives. After each state there are two numbers: the first is the number of members who have served more than ten terms, and the second is the number of those who have served between five and nine terms.

1. To calculate the "seniority rating" for any state, perform the following steps. First, take the first number and multiply by 10. Then take the second number and multiply by 7. Add the two numbers. Then divide that sum by the total number of members of the House from that state. To find the number of representatives in a state, consult *The Congressional Directory* or Barone's *Almanac of American Politics*. Note that the number of representatives is likely to be considerably larger than the number who have served for more than five terms.

2. Once you have learned to calculate the "seniority ratings" for states, you can:
   a. Compare one state with another to see which has the advantage.
   b. Compare a state in 1977–1978 with subsequent or prior years, using past editions of *The Congressional Directory* or the *Almanac* to see if the state is increasing its seniority.
   c. Compare regions by amalgamating totals for several states.

3. You can test the theory that southern states, because of the one-party system in the South, have disproportionate seniority in the House. Compute the ratings for the eleven southern states (Alabama, Arkansas, Florida, Georgia,

TABLE 6.3 State Seniority in the House of Representatives (as of 1978–1979)

Alabama	0/6*		Montana	0/0
Alaska	0/0		Nebraska	0/0
Arizona	1/1		Nevada	0/0
Arkansas	0/2		New Hampshire	0/1
California	5/16		New Jersey	2/5
Colorado	0/1		New Mexico	0/1
Connecticut	0/1		New York	2/16
Delaware	0/0		North Carolina	1/3
Florida	4/6		North Dakota	0/1
Georgia	1/1		Ohio	4/9
Hawaii	0/0		Oklahoma	1/0
Idaho	0/0		Oregon	1/0
Illinois	6/7		Pennsylvania	4/6
Indiana	1/3		Rhode Island	0/1
Iowa	1/0		South Carolina	0/1
Kansas	0/3		South Dakota	0/0
Kentucky	2/2		Tennessee	0/3
Louisiana	0/1		Texas	7/8
Maine	0/0		Utah	0/0
Maryland	0/1		Vermont	0/0
Massachusetts	4/2		Virginia	0/4
Michigan	4/6		Washington	0/2
Minnesota	1/1		West Virginia	2/1
Mississippi	1/1		Wisconsin	3/2
Missouri	1/3		Wyoming	0/0

*The first figure is the number of members who have served more than ten terms, and the second is the number who have served between five and nine terms.

Louisiana, Mississippi, North Carolina, South Carolina, Tennessee, Texas, Virginia). Compare these ratings with:
a. The six states of New England (Connecticut, Maine, Massachusetts, New Hampshire, Rhode Island, Vermont).
b. The industrial states of the Northeast and Midwest (New Jersey, New York, Pennsylvania, and Illinois, Indiana, Michigan, Ohio).

4. Members of Congress with the most seniority on committees are almost always chosen as chairmen. In fact, in the 1960s, 100 percent of the seniority leaders were chosen chairmen. Since 1974 the inflexible "rule of seniority" has been modified by a system in which House Democrats, acting in their party caucus, have at times "overthrown" a seniority leader and given the chairmanship of a committee to someone else. Just how strong is the seniority rule today? You can find out for each session of Congress. Consult

Congressional Quarterly Weekly Reports in every odd-numbered year. Sometime in January a report is made on the action of the Democratic caucus and the full House in choosing committee chairmen. See what happened in January 1981, for example. Were any seniority leaders denied chairmanships? If so, why?

5. Political scientists in the 1950s and 1960s argued that because of the seniority rule the South was "overrepresented" in proportion to its share of the population in committee chairmanships in the House and Senate. You can see if any region of the nation is overrepresented today by consulting *Congressional Quarterly Weekly Reports* in late January of each odd-numbered year for a listing of committee assignments for each member of the House and Senate. You can also use *The Congressional Directory* to obtain a listing of each committee and subcommittee chairmanship in the House and Senate. How did your state do? Add up the number of committee and subcommittee chairmanships. Compute the "expected number" which you can obtain by the following ratio:

$$\frac{\text{number of Democrats from your state in the chamber}}{\text{number of Democrats in the chamber}} \div \frac{\text{"expected number"}}{\text{number of chairmanships in the chamber}}$$

To calculate this ratio, do the following steps. First, multiply the number of Democrats from your state in the chamber by the number of chairmanships in the chamber. Next, divide by the number of Democrats in the chamber. The result should equal the "expected number."

You may also do this for other states. Do you think the largest states like New York, Pennsylvania, Illinois, California, and Texas have adequate representation? Consider especially the representation of large states in Senate chairmanships.

6. Committee chairmen and the ranking minority members on committees have served many terms in the House. It has been argued that members can only serve many terms if they come from districts that are not very competitive. Therefore, committee leaders are the most insulated from electoral competition, since most come from safe seats. You can test this hypothesis by examining the chairmen and ranking minority members in the House standing committees in 1981–1982. Table 6.4 lists these members of Congress with the percentage of the vote they obtained in the last congressional elections.

   a. How many chairs or ranking members come from competitive districts? (A competitive district is normally defined as one in which the incumbent receives less than 55 percent of the vote.) How many chairs or ranking members received more than twice as many votes as all opponents?

   b. Calculate the mean percentage in Table 6.4 for Democratic chairmen

TABLE 6.4 Electoral Competition and Committee Leadership, 1981

Democratic Committee Chairs		Republican Ranking Minority Members	
de la Garza	70.3	Wampler	69
Whitten	62.8	Conte	75
Price	64	Dickinson	61.6
St. Germain	68	Stanton	71
Jones	58	Latta	70
Dellums	56	McKinney	62
Perkins	100	Ashbrook	73
Dingell	70	Broyhill	70
Zablocki	70	Broomfield	72
Brooks	100	Horton	72
Udall	58	Lujan	51
Rodino	86	McClory	72
Jones	100	Snyder	67
Ford	68	Derwinski	68
Howard	50	Clausen	55
Bolling	70	Quillen	87
Fuqua	71	Winn	57
Mitchell	89	McDade	76
Montgomery	100	Hammerschmidt	100
Rostenkowski	84	Conable	72

and Republican ranking members. Usually Democratic mean percents are slightly higher than Republican ones.

   c. Consider the consequences of these percentages. Is it likely that insulated incumbents will be immediately responsive to changing public opinion? Is it likely that such members will want to respond to pressures put on them by their own party caucuses? Is it likely that these Democratic committee leaders will feel it necessary to respond to the bidding of a Republican president, even if that president commands widespread public support for parts of his program? If not, why not?

7. The more prestigious and powerful the committee, the more likely it is that members with seniority will take positions on it. This means that the entire membership of some of the most important House committees consists of members so entrenched in their districts that they resemble the committee chairmen and ranking minority members of the whole House. You can prove this to yourself by examining two of the most powerful House committees, Ways and Means and Appropriations.

   The following are the percentages achieved by the Democratic members of Ways and Means in the 1980 elections: 84, 72, 59, 97, 63, 55, 58, 57, 100,

87, 69, 67, 78, 56, 80, 74, 65, 66, 69, 64, 93, 71, 68. The Republican members of Ways and Means received the following percentages: 72, 76, 83, 97, 74, 76, 58, 79, 76, 76, 71, 100. Calculate the mean percentage for each party.

To find the percentages for members on the House Appropriations Committee, obtain the roster of the committee from the 1981 *Congressional Directory.* Then find the election results for these members in the *Congressional Quarterly Almanac,* 1980, pp. B-23 through B-30.

Are most members of these two powerful committees from competitive districts? Consider the consequences of such electoral insulation on the membership of such committees. Can these figures provide a clue as to why presidential tax measures are so often modified in the House Ways and Means Committee? Why are presidential budget requests modified?

President Reagan won support from Republican members of both committees for his tax and budget proposals. Do you think these members supported the president because they needed his supported in future House elections? If not, what other reasons can you think of that might explain their loyalty?

EXERCISE 7

Presidential Power

Political scientists have been ambivalent about the size and responsibilities of the White House Office and the Executive Office of the President. As you have learned in Chapter 11, the responsibilities of the presidency have expanded in modern times, and the size and complexity of the "institutionalized" presidency have kept pace. In the 1960s most political scientists approved of the enlargement of the president's personal staff and of the increase in presidential agencies. Only a decade later many of the same commentators warned against the "palace guard" mentality of staff members, intent on buffering the president from outside influences and preserving their own personal power. As part of the critique against the "imperial presidency" of the Vietnam and Watergate period, political scientists now recommended a reduction in the size of the White House Office (the personal staff) and of the Executive Office of the President (the presidential agencies).

A. Organizing the Presidency

You can find out the size and functions of the present White House staff by doing some of the following projects.

1. To determine the size of the White House Office consult the *Budget of the United States Government, Appendix*, under the heading "Executive Office of the President." There you will find that the president receives $250,000 in

salary, and that the White House Office in 1977 consisted of 458 permanent positions at a cost of $16,657,000. The Carter administration in 1977 planned to cut the number of positions by 1979 to 351 with a cost of $16,907,000 (indicating rather large increases in salaries for a smaller sized staff). If you consult the latest *Appendix* of the budget, you can determine if the Carter administration succeeded in reducing the size of the White House Office. In the 1982 budget *Appendix* you can see if President Reagan increased or decreased the White House staff.

2. The *Appendix* also provides information on presidential agencies in the Executive Office of the President. Table 7.1 presents information from the *Appendix* for 1977. Add the totals in each column. Can Carter claim to have

TABLE 7.1 Agency Expenditures: Executive Office of the President (thousands of dollars)

Agency	FY 1977 actual	FY 1978 est.	FY 1979 est.
Council of Economic Advisers	$1,831	$2,018	$2,042
Council on Environmental Quality	3,199	2,854	3,126
Council on International Economic Policy	1,012	—	—
Council on Wage and Price Stability	1,762	1,781	1,760
Domestic Council (Domestic Staff)	1,532	2,684	2,630
National Security Council	3,256	3,155	3,432
Office of Administration	—	6,672	8,872
Office of Drug Abuse Policy	954	429	—
Office of Management and Budget	26,762	25,842	28,146
Office of Science and Technology	2,201	2,800	2,621
Office of Special Representative for Trade Negotiations	2,621	2,751	2,665
Office of Telecommunications Policy	8,407	2,112	—

made a start in paring down the size of the Executive Office of the President? Use the 1981 budget *Appendix* and compare the actual figures for 1978 and 1979 with the estimated figures presented here. How well did the White House do in forecasting its own costs? In controlling increases of expenditures for its own operations?

3. An indispensable source for finding the table of organization for each government agency is the *United States Government Organization Manual.* It provides information about the most important officials in each department, including their office addresses. It also provides information about the White House Office and the Executive Office of the President. Obtain the latest volume of this manual. Turn to the listing "White House Office." You can find the names and positions of the most important presidential advisers. You can also determine whether or not the number of senior aides has been increasing or decreasing, and whether substantive experts or campaign and media specialists predominate among the presidential advisers.

In 1971, for example, the Nixon White House included: 2 counsellors, 6 assistants, 2 counsel, 2 advisers, 3 special consultants, 1 director, 1 press secretary, 1 military assistant, 4 special counsel, 5 deputy assistants, 2 deputy press secretaries, 1 personal secretary, and 15 special assistants, for a total of 45 senior aides.

In 1978, after claiming a reduction in the size of the overall White House Office, Carter had assistants with the following titles: 8 assistants, 1 counsel, 1 press secretary, 1 secretary to the cabinet, 14 special assistants, 1 appointments secretary, 1 personal assistant, 1 counsellor, 9 deputy assistants, 2 deputies to assistants, 1 deputy secretary to the cabinet, 2 deputy press secretaries, 1 deputy counsel, 1 director of White House projects, 1 director of White House military office, 2 senior associate counsel, 1 chief speechwriter, 1 director of the personnel office, 1 director of White House operations, 2 associates for intergovernmental affairs, 1 staff secretary, 4 associate press secretaries, 1 deputy appointments secretary, 1 counsel to the Intelligence Oversight Board, 1 associate counsel, 1 editor of news summary, 1 director of the Office of Presidential Messages, 3 speechwriters, 2 associate directors of the personnel office, 1 director of the Visitor's Office, and 1 director of advance, for a total of 69 senior positions.

Consult the latest edition of the *United States Government Organization Manual.* Has the number of White House aides continued to increase? How would you characterize most of the positions? Are they primarily political, involving the president's communication with various groups, or do most White House duties involve substantive administrative responsibilities?

4. Agencies in the Executive Office of the President have different functions. Some advise the president; others coordinate programs in the departments; others perform staff functions like budgeting or personnel; and still others are "line" agencies that belong in the departments, but for one reason or another were placed in the presidential office. In the 1960s this last category

of "line" agencies accounted for much of the increase in the presidential office. Agencies designed to fight poverty, end drug abuse, take care of senior citizens, or promote the maritime industry all found their way into the Executive Office of the President instead of being placed in departments where they belonged. In the 1970s the Nixon, Ford, and Carter administrations pledged to reorganize the presidential office and remove these agencies.

To study the structure of the Executive Office of the President, consult the *United States Government Organization Manual.* Figure 7.1 shows the various offices of the Nixon administration in 1971. Using the latest *Manual* answer the following questions: To what extent does the White House still retain "line" agencies, which seem to you to belong in departments? Which agencies do you believe are the most important to the president, based on the descriptions of their functions contained in the *Manual*? Do you have any candidates for agencies that might usefully be transferred to departments?

You might be interested to know that one of the reasons why the White House Office has reduced its size in recent years is that many of its functions have been transferred to the new Office of Administration located in the

FIGURE 7.1   The Executive Office of the President, 1971

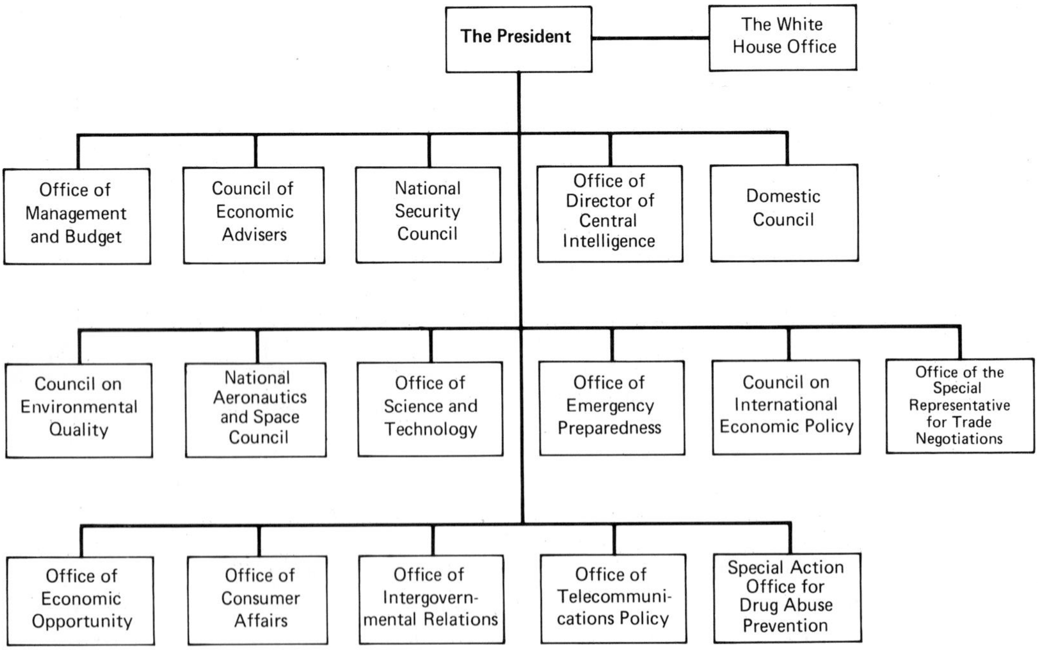

Executive Office. Therefore, it is somewhat misleading to assume that the total size of the "presidential" staff has decreased, since many of the functions have been shifted from one office to the other.

5. To follow developments involving the White House Office and the Executive Office of the President, consult the weekly periodical *The National Journal*, which covers the executive branch. In the early stages of each new administration, this magazine carries stories on planned reorganizations, and also reports the changes actually made by each president to make the institutionalized presidency more responsive to his own operating style. You might find it especially interesting to do a research paper comparing the Nixon and Carter reorganizations.

B. Presidential Popularity

Presidents and political commentators alike are always interested in how the incumbent is faring in the public opinion surveys. Every president begins his term with high ratings during the "honeymoon" period. Each (with the exception of Eisenhower) experienced a decline in his approval rating, with a slight "rebound" effect near the end of his term. In spite of the long-term decline every president faces, there are occasional short-term "bursts" based on a favorable development or international crisis, or a short-term "collapse" based on a highly unpopular action (like Ford's pardon of Nixon).

1. Table 7.2 gives the results of Gallup Polls for Nixon, Ford, Carter, and Reagan, showing the percent of respondents who expressed approval of each president. If your library has the *Gallup Opinion Index* for 1978 and subsequent years, complete the table for the Carter and Reagan presidencies. To what extent does it seem that presidents "slide" in popularity dramatically? To what extent does the "rebound" effect exist near the end of their terms? Do you think that presidents have been popular leaders in recent administrations?

2. There are many criticisms of how polls to measure presidential popularity are conducted. Some political scientists believe that the results of the Harris and Gallup polls may not be accurate. The following selection, by Gary Orren, a professor at Harvard University, assesses the two leading commercial polls.

TABLE 7.2 Gallup Approval Scores for Nixon, Ford, Carter, and Reagan (in percentages)

NIXON				FORD		CARTER		REAGAN	
1969		**1973**		**1974**		**1977**		**1981**	
Feb. 9	59	Jan. 15	51	Aug. 19	71	Feb. 7	66	early Feb.	51
Mar. 2	61	Jan. 29	68	Sept. 9	66	Mar. 7	70	mid-Feb.	55
Mar. 30	65	Feb. 19	65	Sept. 30	50	Apr. 4	67	mid-Mar.	60
May 1	61	Mar. 30	59	Oct. 14	52	May 9	66		
May 18	64	Apr. 9	54	Oct. 18	55	June 6	63		
June 5	65	Apr. 30	48	Nov. 11	47	July 11	62		
July 6	63	May 7	45	Nov. 18	48	Aug. 8	60		
Aug. 10	65	May 14	44	Dec. 9	42	Sept. 12	54		
Aug. 28	62	June 4	44			Oct. 3	59		
Sept. 30	60	June 25	45	**1975**		Nov. 7	55		
Oct. 16	57	July 9	40	Jan. 13	37	Dec. 12	57		
Nov. 23	68	Aug. 6	31	Jan. 31	39				
		Aug. 19	38	Feb. 28	39	**1978**			
1970		Sept. 10	35	Apr. 18	39	early Jan.	55		
Jan. 18	61	Sept. 24	32	June 2	51	late Feb.	50		
Feb. 12	66	Oct. 8	30	June 30	52	mid-Mar.	50		
July 12	59	Oct. 22	27	Aug. 4	45	mid-Apr.	40		
July 30	61	Nov. 5	27	Aug. 18	46	mid-May	43		
Aug. 20	55	Dec. 3	31	Sept. 12	47	mid-June	42		
Sept. 13	56	Dec. 10	29	Oct. 6	47	late July	39		
Nov. 29	57			Oct. 20	47	late Aug.	43		
Dec. 17	52	**1974**		Nov. 3	34	late Sept.	48		
		Jan. 7	27	Nov. 24	41	mid-Oct.	49		
1971		Jan. 21	26	Dec. 8	46	mid-Nov.	50		
Jan. 10	56	Feb. 11	27	Dec. 15	39	mid-Dec.	51		
Mar. 4	51	Mar. 4	25						
Apr. 1	50	Mar. 18	26	**1976**		**1979**			
June 11	48	Apr. 1	26	Jan. 5	46	mid-Jan.	43		
July 11	48	Apr. 15	25	Jan. 26	45	late Feb.	37		
Sept. 13	49	May 13	25	Feb. 27	48	mid-Mar.	47		
Oct. 8	54	June 3	28	Mar. 21	50	mid-Apr.	40		
Nov. 18	49	June 24	26	Apr. 12	48	mid-May	32		
Nov. 26	50	Aug. 5	24	May 24	47	late June	29		
Dec. 23	49			June 14	45	mid-July	29		
				Dec. 13	53	mid-Aug.	33		
1972						mid-Sept.	30		
Jan. 12	49					mid-Oct.	31		
Feb. 7	53					mid-Nov.	38		
Feb. 20	56					late Nov.	51		
Mar. 27	53					early Dec.	61		
May 29	61								
June 19	56					**1980**			
Dec. 19	62					mid-Jan	58		
						late Feb.	52		
						late Mar.	39		
						mid-Apr.	39		
						mid-May	38		
						mid-June	32		
						mid-July	33		
						mid-Aug.	32		
						mid-Sept.	37		
						mid-Nov.	31		
						mid-Dec.	34		

Sources: *Gallup Poll Index*, 1935–1971, *Gallup Opinion Index*, 1972–1978, and The Gallup Poll

Presidential Popularity Ratings: Another View

Amidst the avalanche of polling data which fill our newspapers and air waves daily, none commands more attention than the periodic reports of presidential popularity.

Unfortunately, the two most prominent measures of presidential popularity, the Gallup and Harris ratings, not only frequently diverge—a point long recognized by political scientists—but also yield an incomplete and perhaps even misleading picture of the public's evaluation.

Noting these longstanding dissimilarities, the *Washington Post* last January asked a national sample of 1,519 adults to rate President Carter's job performance in three different ways—using the Harris question, the Gallup questions, and a new question devised by the *Post*.

The results of the *Post* survey indicate two essential problems with the Harris and Gallup questions: they force people to express firm negative or positive views on the President when, in fact, many respondents have neutral, mixed or uncertain feelings, and the ambiguity of their available choices distorts the usual interpretation of the results. Harris, for instance, offers respondents four choices—whether the President's performance is excellent, pretty good, only fair or poor—and then judges all those who say "only fair" or "poor" as disapprovers." Yet when the *Post* asked the people who rated Carter as "only fair" (in the Harris poll question) whether they actually "approved" or "disapproved" (in the Gallup question), it found that fully 45 percent actually approved of the President's performance. In other words, a large number of people who are counted in the negative column by Harris are put in the positive column by Gallup.

The *Post* explored the problem further by asking people to grade the President's job performance as either "A, B, C, D, or F," thus allowing intermediate responses somewhere between outright approval or disapproval. What it found was that a majority (55 percent) of those who gave an "only fair" answer to the Harris question thought Carter deserved a grade of "C"—arguably, neither favorable nor unfavorable. And when responses to the Gallup question are compared to the *Post* grading scale, the *mildly* approving or disapproving answers also reveal little conviction.

Among all the respondents surveyed in January by the *Post*, the Gallup popularity question put Carter's rating at 63-29 positive; the Harris question among those same respondents put his rating at 48-49 negative; while the *Post* question showed that 41 percent gave him a grade of "A" or "B"; 35 percent gave him a grade of "C," and 17 percent gave him a grade of "D" or "F." The *Post* survey suggests, then, that Harris ratings tend to deflate presidential authority, while the Gallup formulation, which compels people to choose between outright approval or disapproval, often inflates it.

Reprinted with permission from *Public Opinion*, May/June 1978. © The American Enterprise Institute, 1978.

HARRIS vs. GALLUP

The Harris Question:

How would you rate the job Jimmy Carter is doing as President? Would you say he is doing an excellent, pretty good, only fair, or a poor job?

Those who gave Carter a Harris rating of:

Excellent
(5%)

Pretty good
(43%)

Only fair
(40%)

Poor
(9%)

Don't know
(3%)

The Gallup Question:

Do you approve or disapprove of the way Jimmy Carter is handling his job as President? Is that approve/disapprove strongly, or approve/disapprove somewhat?

Gave him a Gallup rating of:

Approval
Disapproval
Don't know

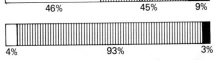
94%   3% 3%

90%   6% 4%

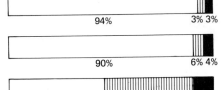
46%   45%   9%

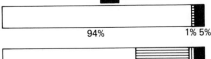
4%   93%   3%

30%   7%   63%

HARRIS vs. THE POST

The Harris Question:

How would you rate the job Jimmy Carter is doing as President? Would you say he is doing an excellent, pretty good, only fair, or a poor job?

Those who gave Carter a Harris rating of:

Excellent
(5%)

Pretty good
(43%)

Only fair
(40%)

Poor
(9%)

Don't know
(3%)

The Washington Post Question:

Suppose you were to grade President Carter A, B, C, D or F for the way he is handling his job as President. What grade would you give him?

Gave him a Post grade of:

A–B
C
D–F
Don't know

94%   1% 5%

64%   28%   3% 5%

19%   55%   21%   5%

3% 7%   85%   5%

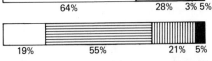

18%   16% 7%   59%

The *Post* question itself surely suffers from certain deficiencies. Respondents are naturally attracted to a middle position like "C." Moreover, without additional evidence one cannot interpret the precise meaning of the "C" grade: to some citizens it represents a mediocre or average rating, to others it is an expression of uncertainty. Still, it is undoubtedly true that many people—though perhaps not all—who gave Carter a "C" do in fact fall into the middle.

A familiar rebuttal to this argument against current popularity ratings is that any *single* number from Gallup or Harris is not critical—the thing to watch is the trend line, and for that purpose, the present questions are valid. This rebuttal rests on the assumption that imperfect questions introduce a constant random bias, which can safely be ignored in comparisons over time. However, the bias introduced by the poor wording of questions is neither random nor constant. As we have seen, for example, respondents who are ignored by the Harris and Gallup questions—those with neutral views—do *not* split evenly into approvers and disapprovers. Since the proportion of people holding neutral views changes over time, the amount of distortion also varies.

The impact of presidential popularity ratings is far too great for us simply to conclude with a call for more humility and caution in interpreting poll results. Valid interpretation of public opinion on a single issue requires a variety of questions with different formats and alternative wordings. Economists, for example, have long relied on an assortment of indicators and composite indexes for appraising the performance of the economy.

Yet until now, cost-conscious polling agencies have eschewed such "academic" approaches in measuring something even more elusive, presidential performance. Just as wars are too important to leave to the generals, presidential popularity may be imperiled in the hands of commercial pollsters, unless they amend their ways.

3. You might find it interesting to try to incorporate the criticisms made by Orren in the construction of your own poll. The following, which appeared in the Columbia University student newspaper shows how a poll of student opinion can be conducted.

A Student Opinion Poll

Students are generally noncommittal about President Carter, a poll of 70 Barnard and [Columbia] college students revealed, with the majority approving of his foreign policies and disagreeing with the way he is handling domestic issues.

On a scale of "very good, fairly good, just OK, fairly bad, and bad," Carter's overall performance was rated "just OK" by 47 percent of the students.

Reprinted from David Glass, "Poll Shows Disapproval of Carter," *Columbia Daily Spectator*, December 11, 1978. Used by permission.

A little over 16 percent rated Carter as "fairly good," and in an increase of 20 percent from a similar poll taken last year, 36 percent said he is "fairly bad."

The poll, which was taken after the Thanksgiving weekend, showed that Carter is doing "fairly badly" in domestic affairs, according to 34 percent of the students, and "badly," according to 15 percent. Thirty-nine percent liked Carter's performance in foreign affairs, the same percentage he received last year.

Twenty-seven percent of those interviewed voted for Carter in 1976, 10 percent voted for Ford, 20 percent voted for fringe or write-in candidates, and 43 percent did not vote.

Generally, students expressed doubt about Carter's performance. College student Ronald Madena called Carter "another Jerry Ford." Most called his energy program "a joke," and were critical of his anti-inflation policies, calling them "soft."

According to the poll, Carter's strongest area is foreign affairs. Fifty-one percent reacted positively to his policies toward the Soviet Union, and 78 percent liked what he is doing in the Middle East.

Significantly, there was very little criticism of Carter's call for a Palestinian homeland, a subject which enraged many people last year. The feeling now is that "as long as there is peace, I am happy," as one Barnard student said who did not want to identify herself.

Carter's domestic policy is hurting him most, the poll revealed. Forty-three percent rated his energy program as "fairly bad." Aaron Abrowitz called his programs "a lot of talk with no substance." The majority of the students thought the energy problem was important, but the urgency surrounding the issue in recent years has diminished.

On the economy, Carter has fared poorly. Twenty-six percent rated him as "fairly bad" while 22 percent gave him the worst rating possible. Carter's employment rating was somewhat better. Fifty-four percent rated him either good or "OK," with only 13 percent rating him "bad."

An interesting turnabout came in students' perceptions of Carter's stand on abortion. Most were unaware that he did have a stand on abortion, while those who knew he was against it approved by a 54 to 46 percent ratio.

On balance, students are not impressed with Carter, although 67 percent thought he would be reelected in 1980. Among other Democratic candidates, Massachusetts Senator Edward Kennedy was the overwhelming favorite. Inconsistently, the majority of those who said they voted for Carter now favored Kennedy for the 1980 election, while at the same time saying they expected the President would be reelected.

4. Since public opinion polls survey only a "sample" of the population, there is only a *probability* that the opinions of the sample will accurately reflect the opinions of the population at large. You can determine what the probability is that the data in a nationally drawn sample are accurate, based on the number of interviews conducted for the poll. Here is how to perform the calculations.

First, take your calculator and enter .25. Next, divide by the number of interviews conducted for the poll. Now find the square root of that result. Finally, multiply that square root result by 196. The number on your calculator is the margin of error, plus or minus, which should exist for 95 percent of any samples drawn to measure the opinions of the population.

You can understand this calculation by applying it to the survey conducted by the *Washington Post* that is described on page 194 of this Handbook. First, enter .25 on the calculator. Now divide by the number in the sample, 1,519. Find the square root of the result, and multiply by 196. Your answer should be 2.5. This means that every percentage in the survey has an error factor of 2.5 percent, and that the margin of error has a 95 percent probability of being accurate for the nationwide adult population that is represented by the sample polled.

5. You should perform this calculation for other national polls to see how accurate their findings are. For example, if a poll had only 500 respondents, what would be the margin of error? Would that margin make it less likely that the poll provided accurate information on presidential popularity or on which candidate was ahead in a campaign?

C. How Textbooks Deal with the Presidency

In the 1960s most college textbooks in political science glorified the presidency as an instrument of democracy, and tended to ignore or gloss over the problems involved in the system of "presidential government." The following selection by political scientist Thomas Cronin indicates why the traditional textbook treatment was unsatisfactory in providing students with a realistic assessment of the powers and functions of the office.

Ascriptions of Power and Virtue

With minor variations college texts of the 1950s and 1960s stressed that the contemporary presidency was growing dramatically larger, gaining significantly more resources and responsibilities. This expansion was often described metaphorically as "wearing more hats." With rare exception texts not only devised and approved but openly celebrated an expansive theory of presidential power. Students read that more authority and discretion in determining policy devolves to the president during war and crises and that because the country was engaged in sustained international conflict and acute

From Thomas E. Cronin, *The State of the Presidency*, 2nd ed., pp. 78–81, 83–84. Copyright © 1980 by Thomas E. Cronin. Reprinted by permission of the publisher, Little, Brown and Company.

domestic problems, presidents were constantly becoming more powerful. One text pointed out, "as the world grows smaller, he will grow bigger." Another exclaimed that the "President . . . bears almost the entire burden of the formulation of national policy and the definition of the national purpose." The following presidential job descriptions have been taken from five of these introductory texts:

The president is the most strategic policy maker in the government. His policy role is paramount in military and foreign affairs.

He [John F. Kennedy] also became the most important and powerful executive in the free world. His powers are so vast that they rival those of the Soviet Premier or any other dictator. He is the chief architect of the nation's public policy; as President, he is one who proposes, requests, supports, demands, and insists that Congress enact most of the major legislation that it does.

The evolution of the Presidency is the story of a frequent and cumulative increase in the role—or, better, the roles—that the President can play and is expected to play in the American political system, and, more recently, in the world. Every "great" President has left the office somewhat altered and enlarged. The Presidency is like a family dwelling that each new generation alters and enlarges. Confronted by some new need, a President adds on a new room, a new wing; what began as a modest dwelling has become a mansion; every President may not use every room, but the rooms are available in case of need.

The President of the United States of America is, without question, the most powerful elected executive in the world. He is at once the chief formulator of public policy as embodied in legislation, leader of a major political party . . . chief architect of American foreign policy. And his power and responsibility are increasing.

If the President is a king, it is equally clear that he is no mere constitutional monarch. For in an era in which many monarchies all over the world have disappeared, and the power of kings has declined, the power of the President has enormously increased . . . through subtle and usually informal changes, attributable mainly to the fact that the President is the literal embodiment of American mass democracy and . . . the symbol of the pervasive egalitarianism which from the beginning has characterized the emergent forces of the American democratic ideal.

To the teenager or young adult, textbook discussions of the extensive resources available to the president cannot help but convey the impression that a president must have just about all the inside information and good advice anyone could want, especially when they point out the vast arrays of experts, strategic support staffs, and intelligence systems. Usually, too, a lengthy listing is included of the National Security Council, the cabinet, the Office of Management and Budget, the Council on Environmental Quality, the Council of Economic Advisers, White House domestic-policy staffs, and count-

less high-level study commissions. A casual reading of such chapters fosters
the conclusion that a contemporary president can both set and shape the
directions of public policy and can see to it that these policies *work as intended.*

The conviction that the president knows best, and his advisory information
systems are unparalleled, is readily encouraged by a passage like the following:

> *The President has not only the authority but the capacity to act. For
> example, he has at his command unmatched sources of information. To his
> desk come facts channeled from the entire world. Diplomatic missions, military
> observers, undercover agents, personal agents, technical experts gather tons
> of material which are analyzed by experts in the State Department and else-
> where. Since the President draws on the informed thinking of hundreds of
> specialists, his pronouncements have a tone of authority.*

To this vast reservoir is added the capacity of the presidency for systematic
thinking and planning, similarly described as awesome and superbly suited to
the challenges of the day:

> *Presidential government is a superb planning institution. The President
> has the attention of the country, the administrative goals, the command of
> information, and the fiscal resources that are necessary for intelligent plan-
> ning, and he is gaining the institutional power that will make such planning
> operational. Better than any other human instrumentality, he can order the
> relations of his ends and means, alter existing institutions and procedures or
> create new ones, calculate the consequences of different policies, experiment
> with various methods, control the timing of action, anticipate the reactions of
> affected interests, and conciliate them or at least mediate among them.*

This same theme is outlined in Theodore White's *The Making of the President
1960*, often used as a supplementary text: "So many and so able are the
President's advisers of the permanent services of Defense, State, Treasury,
Agriculture, that when crisis happens all necessary information is instantly
available, all alternate courses already plotted." Elsewhere, White pays lavish
tribute to America's "action-intellectuals," whom he designates as the "new
priesthood" of national policy making. These "best and brightest," recruited
from prestigious universities and research centers, are credited with being a
benign and "propelling influence" upon our government, "shaping our de-
fenses, guiding our foreign policy, redesigning our cities, reorganizing our
schools."

Clinton Rossiter's *The American Presidency*, published in 1956 and still
widely read, contains one of the most lucid venerations of the American
presidency. Rossiter describes the presidency sympathetically as a priceless
American invention that not only has worked extremely well but also is a
symbol of the continuity and destiny of the American people.

Few nations have solved so simply and yet grandly the problem of finding and maintaining an office or state that embodies their majesty and reflects their character.

There is virtually no limit to what the President can do if he does it for democratic ends and by democratic means.

He is, rather, a kind of magnificent lion who can roam widely and do great deeds so long as he does not try to break loose from his broad reservation.

He reigns, but he also rules; he symbolizes the people, but he also runs their government.

Rossiter, both fully aware of his own biases and seemingly quite convinced that the myth of presidential greatness and grandeur was to be cultivated, writes about the Lincoln legacy:

Lincoln is the supreme myth, the richest symbol in the American experience. He is, as someone has remarked neither irreverently nor sacrilegiously, the martyred Christ of democracy's passion play. And who, then, can measure the strength that is given to the President because he holds Lincoln's office, lives in Lincoln's house, and walks in Lincoln's way? The final greatness of the Presidency lies in the truth that it is not just an office of incredible power but a breeding ground of indestructible myth.

Such lavish prose hardly discourages awe and admiration, if not exactly reverence, for the presidency.

Perhaps the most respected specialized treatment of the presidency written in the 1950s and 1960s was Richard Neustadt's *Presidential Power* (1960). Neustadt's insights countered much of the conventional wisdom by stressing the highly political and bureaucratic context in which presidents must operate, the obstacles posed to presidential directives by Washington empire builders, and the scarce resources available to a president who wants to reverse policy directions. Although his analysis found the president's position limited and tenuous, one in which he must grasp for just enough power to get by the next day's problems, Neustadt seemed personally to prefer a more powerful president—one who would guard his options and would impose his will. But implicitly, if not explicitly, his study held on to the hope that a shrewd and manipulative leader could and should be a powerful engine of change. Indeed an aggressive, ambitious politician, determined to get his way and ever-distrustful of the motives of others, seemed to be what was needed.

• • •

The personalized presidency is as well a central feature of contemporary political journalism. No one did more to embellish this perspective than Theodore White, whose *Making of the President* volumes not only enjoy frequent university use but also serve as texts for the millions of adults who savor the explanations of an insider. White's concentration on the styles and personalities of the candidates promotes a benevolent, almost liturgical, orientation toward the presidency. His narrative histories have an uncanny knack of creating suspense about the outcome of an election well after it actually took place. The melodramatic style promotes a heightened sense of reverence for the eventual victor akin to that felt for royalty. White first describes the field of seven or eight competing hopefuls, which becomes four or five; eventually the field is narrowed down to two or three national candidates. Finally, one person remains. Clearly, it seems from White's approach, the victor in such a drawn-out and thoroughly patriotic ritual deserves the nation's deepest respect and approval. Moreover, White subtly purifies the victorious candidate. In what must be the classic metamorphosis at the root of the textbook image of the presidency, the individuals who assume the presidency seem to change physically and, it is implied, spiritually. White says about President Kennedy's first days in the White House in 1961: "It was as if there were an echo, here on another level, in the quiet Oval Office, of all the speeches he had made in all the squares and supermarkets of the country. . . . He had won this office and this power by promising such movement to the American people. Now he had to keep the promise. He seemed very little changed in movement or in gracefulness from the candidate—only his eyes had changed—very dark now, very grave, markedly more sunken and lined at the corners than those of the candidate." He writes of Richard Nixon soon after his ascendancy in 1969:

He seemed, as he waved me into the Oval Office, suddenly on first glance a more stocky man than I had known on the campaign rounds. There was a minute of adjustment as he waved me to a sofa in the barren office, poured coffee, put me at ease; then, watching him, I realized that he was not stockier, but, on the contrary, slimmer. What was different was the movement of the body, the sound of the voice, the manner of speaking—for he was calm as I had never seen him before, as if peace had settled on him. In the past Nixon's restless body had been in constant movement as he rose, walked about, hitched a leg over the arm of a chair or gestured sharply with his hands. Now he was in repose, and the repose was in his speech also—more slow, studied, with none of the gear-slippages of name or reference which used to come when he was weary; his hands still moved as he spoke, but the fingers spread gracefully, not punchily or sharply as they used to.

To summarize, four propositions can be singled out as the main elements of the textbook ideal.

Omnipotent-Competent Dimension:

1. The president is *the* strategic catalyst for progress in the American political system and the central figure in the international system as well.
2. Only the president can be the genuine architect of U.S. public policy, and only he, by attacking problems frontally and aggressively and by interpreting his power expansively, can slay the dragons of crisis and be the engine of change to move his nation forward.

Moralistic-Benevolent Dimension:

3. The president must be the nation's personal and moral leader; by symbolizing the past and future greatness of America and radiating inspirational confidence, a president can pull the nation together while directing its people toward fulfillment of the American Dream.

4. If, and only if, the right person is placed in the White House, all will be well; and somehow, whoever is in the White House is the best person for the job—at least for a year or so.

The significance of the textbook presidency is that the whole is greater than the sum of the parts. It presents a cumulative presidential image, a legacy of past glories and impressive performances—the exalted dignity of Lincoln, the Wilsonian eloquence, the robust vitality of the Roosevelts, the benign smile and lasting popularity of Eisenhower, the inspirational spirit of Kennedy, the legislative wizardry of Lyndon Johnson, the globetrotting of the first-term Nixon—which endows the White House with a singular mystique and almost magical qualities. According to this image, the office of the presidency seems to clothe its occupants in strength and dignity, in might and right, and only men of the caliber of Lincoln, the Roosevelts, or Wilson can seize the chalice of opportunity, create the vision, and rally the American public around that vision.

1. Examine Chapter 11 on the presidency in your textbook. Do you think that Professor Wilson has provided you with the kind of "textbook" presidency treatment that Cronin has criticized? To what extent does Wilson's analysis depart from the four "dimensions" described by Cronin?

2. To some extent the presidents of the United States have perpetuated the myths of the presidency in their public addresses. If your library has this volume, read through *Inaugural Addresses of the Presidents of the United States* (Washington, D.C.: U.S. Government Printing Office, 1965). You might wish to examine especially the inaugural address of President John F. Kennedy in 1961 to see if the president described his office in terms of the four "dimensions." (If you cannot obtain that volume, you should be able to read Kennedy's address as printed in the *New York Times*, January 21, 1961, available in your library on microfilm.)

3. To see whether or not the post-Vietnam and post-Watergate atmosphere has affected presidential rhetoric, you might examine some of the major addresses of the Ford and Carter administrations, especially several of the State of the Union addresses. You can find these in the *Weekly Compilation of Presidential Documents, Public Papers of the Presidents of the United States*, or reprinted in the *New York Times* and available on microfilm.

EXERCISE 8

Implementing Judicial Decisions

When the Supreme Court announces its decision in a case, the result is not self-executing. The original parties to the cause may be immediately affected, but whether or not a decision is implemented in other similar circumstances is a *political* decision. In some circumstances implementation follows immediately and fully, as when the Court ordered President Truman to return steel mills the government had seized during a strike to ensure production for the Korean War, or when the White House complied with a decision requiring it to turn over the "Nixon tapes" to the Watergate special prosecutor.

At the other extreme, a judicial doctrine may give rise to massive resistance and disobedience, an example of which was the flouting of the decisions of the Court dealing with desegregation of public schools in the South in the 1950s. Often there is neither full compliance nor massive resistance, but rather a process of reinterpretation of judicial decisions by officials at all levels of government. If, as one chief justice once remarked, "We are a government under the Constitution, but the Constitution is what the Supreme Court says it is," it may also be added that we govern according to Supreme Court decisions, but these decisions are what public officials and private citizens will make of them.

You can begin to learn about the politics of implementation by following the consequences of the case *Regents of the University of California* v. *Bakke*, a case dealing with admissions policies in professional schools, decided by the Supreme Court on June 28, 1978. To acquaint you with the facts of one of the most important civil rights cases ever decided by the Supreme Court read the syllabus of the case that was prepared by the Court's reporter of decisions.

Syllabus of *Regents of the University of California v. Bakke*

The Medical School of the University of California at Davis (hereinafter Davis) had two admissions programs for the entering class of 100 students—the regular admissions program and the special admissions program. Under the regular procedure, candidates whose overall undergraduate grade point averages fell below 2.5 on a scale of 4.0 were summarily rejected. About one out of six applicants was then given an interview, following which he was rated on a scale of 1 to 100 by each of the committee members (five in 1973 and six in 1974), his rating being based on the interviewers' summaries, his overall grade point average, his science courses grade point average, and his Medical College Admissions Test (MCAT) scores, letters of recommendation, extracurricular activities, and other biographical data, all of which resulted in a total "benchmark score." The full admissions committee then made offers of admission on the basis of their review of the applicant's file and his score, considering and acting upon applications as they were received. The committee chairman was responsible for placing names on the waiting list and had discretion to include persons with "special skills." A separate committee, a majority of whom were members of minority groups, operated the special admissions program. The 1973 and 1974 application forms, respectively, asked candidates whether they wished to be considered as "economically and/or educationally disadvantaged" applicants and members of a "minority group" (blacks, Chicanos, Asians, American Indians). If an applicant of a minority group was found to be "disadvantaged," he would be rated in a manner similar to the one employed by the general admissions committee. Special candidates, however, did not have to meet the 2.5 grade point cut-off and were not ranked against candidates in the general admissions process. About one-fifth of the special applicants were invited for interviews in 1973 and 1974, following which they were given benchmark scores, and the top choices were then given to the general admissions committee, which could reject special candidates for failure to meet course requirements or other specific deficiencies. The special committee continued to recommend candidates until 16 special admission selections had been made. During a four-year period 63 minority students were admitted to Davis under the special program and 44 under the general program. No disadvantaged whites were admitted under the special program, though many applied. Respondent, a white male, applied to Davis in 1973 and 1974, in both years being considered only under the general admissions program. Though he had a 468 out of 500 score in 1973, he was rejected since no general applicants with scores less than 470 were being accepted after respondent's application, which was filed late in the year, had been processed and completed. At that time four special admission slots were still unfilled. In 1974 respondent applied early, and though he had a total score of 549 out of 600, he was again rejected. In neither year was his name placed on the discretionary waiting list. In both years special applicants were admitted with significantly lower scores than respondent's. After his second rejection, respondent filed this action in state court for mandatory injunctive and declaratory relief to compel his admission to Davis, alleging that the special admissions program operated to exclude him on the basis of his race in violation of the Equal Protection Clause of the Fourteenth Amendment, a provision of the California Constitution, and § 601 of Title VI of the Civil Rights Act of 1964, which provides, *inter alia*, that no person shall on the ground of race or color be excluded from participating in any program receiving federal financial assistance. Petitioner cross-claimed for a declaration that its special admissions program was lawful. The trial court found that the special program operated as a racial quota, because minority applicants in that program were rated only against one another, and 16 places in the class of 100 were reserved for them. Declaring that petitioner could not take race into account in making admissions decisions, the program was held to violate the Federal and State Constitutions and Title VI. Respondent's admission was not ordered, however, for lack of proof that he would have been admitted but for the special program. The California Supreme Court, applying a strict-scrutiny standard, concluded that the special admissions program was not the least intrusive means of achieving the goals of the admittedly compelling state interests of integrating the medical profession and increasing the number of doctors willing to serve minority patients. Without passing on the state constitutional or federal statutory grounds the court held that petitioner's special admissions program violated the Equal Protection Clause. Since petitioner could not satisfy its burden of demonstrating that respondent, absent the special program, would not have been admitted, the court ordered his admission to Davis.

Held: The judgment below is affirmed insofar as it orders respondent's admission to Davis and invalidates petitioner's special admissions program, but is reversed insofar as it prohibits petitioner from taking race into account as a factor in its future admissions decisions.

Justice Lewis Powell, writing the decision of the Supreme Court, struck down the admission procedures of the University of California at Davis, and ordered the admission of Allan Bakke. At the same time, the Court also upheld the use of race as a criterion in admission for the purposes of affirmative action. By upholding the principle of affirmative action while striking down a particular program because it created a rigid quota system, the Court left open the question of what kinds of programs it would permit, and what kinds it would strike down.

Reprinted below are excerpts from the *Bakke* case that are of particular interest to college and professional school admissions officers who are required to design an affirmative action admissions program in the aftermath of the decision.

Regents of the University of California v. Bakke

JUSTICE POWELL:

The parties fight a sharp preliminary action over the proper characterization of the special admissions program. Petitioner prefers to view it as establishing a "goal" of minority representation in the medical school. Respondent, echoing the courts below, labels it a racial quota.

This semantic distinction is beside the point: the special admissions program is undeniably a classification based on race and ethnic background.

The guarantees of the 14th Amendment extend to persons. Its language is explicit: "No state shall deny to any person within its jurisdiction the equal protection of the laws."

The guarantee of equal protection cannot mean one thing when applied to one individual and something else when applied to a person of another color. If both are not accorded the same protection, then it is not equal. Racial and ethnic distinctions of any sort are inherently suspect and thus call for the most exacting judicial examination.

· · ·

We have held that in "order to justify the use of a suspect classification, a state must show that its purpose or interest is both constitutionally permissible and substantial and that its use of the classification is 'necessary to the accomplishment' of its purpose or the safeguarding of its interest."

The special admissions program purports to serve the purposes of: (i) "reducing the historic deficit of traditionally disfavored minorities in medical schools and the medical profession"; (ii) countering the effects of societal discrimination; (iii) increasing the number of physicians who will practice in communities currently underserved; and (iv) obtaining the educational benefits that flow from an ethnically diverse student body. It is necessary to decide which, if any, of these purposes is substantial enough to support the use of a suspect classification.

If petitioner's purpose is to assure within its student body some specified percentage of a particular group merely because of its race or ethnic origin, such a preferential purpose must be rejected not as insubstantial but as facially invalid. Preferring members of any one group for no reason other than race or ethnic origin is discrimination for its own sake. This the Constitution forbids.

The state certainly has a legitimate and substantial interest in ameliorating, or eliminating where feasible, the disabling effects of identified discrimination.

We have never approved a classification that aids persons perceived as members of relatively victimized groups at the expense of other innocent individuals in the absence of judicial, legislative or administrative findings of constitutional or statutory violations.

· · ·

The fourth goal asserted by petitioner is the attainment of a diverse student body. This clearly is a constitutionally permissible goal for an institution of higher education. Academic freedom, though not a specifically enumerated constitutional right, long has been viewed as a special concern of the First Amendment. The freedom of a university to make its own judgments as to education includes the selection of its student body.

· · ·

It may be argued that there is greater force to these views at the under-graduate level than in a medical school where the training is centered primarily on professional competency. But even at the graduate level, our tradition and experience lend support to the view that the contribution of diversity is substantial.

Ethnic diversity, however, is only one element in a range of factors a university properly may consider in attaining the goal of a heterogeneous student body. Although a university must have wide discretion in making the sensitive judgments as to who should be admitted, constitutional limitations protecting individual rights may not be disregarded.

Respondent urges—and the courts below have held—that petitioner's dual admissions program is a racial classification that impermissibly infringes his rights under the 14th Amendment. As the interest of diversity is compelling in the context of a university's admissions program, the question remains whether the program's racial classification is necessary to promote this interest.

•　　•　　•

The experience of other university admissions programs, which take race into account in achieving the educational diversity valued by the First Amendment, demonstrates that the assignment of a fixed number of places to a minority group is not a necessary means toward that end. An illuminating example is found in the Harvard College program:

"In recent years Harvard College has expanded the concept of diversity to include students from disadvantaged economic, racial and ethnic groups. Harvard College now recruits not only Californians or Louisianans but also blacks and Chicanos and other minority students.

"In practice, this new definition of diversity has meant that race has been a factor in some admission decisions. When the committee on admissions reviews the large middle group of applicants who are 'admissible' and deemed capable of doing good work in their courses, the race of an applicant may tip the balance in his favor just as geographic origin or a life spent on a farm may tip the balance in other candidates' cases. A farm boy from Idaho can bring something to Harvard College that a Bostonian cannot offer. Similarly, a black student can usually bring something that a white person cannot offer.

"In Harvard College admissions the committee has not set target quotas for the number of blacks, or of musicians, football players, physicists or Californians to be admitted in a given year. But that awareness does not mean that the committee sets the minimum number of blacks or of people from west of the Mississippi who are to be admitted. It means only that in choosing among thousands of applicants who are not only 'admissible' academically but have other strong qualities, the committee, with a number of criteria in mind, pays some attention to distribution among many types and categories of students."

In such an admissions program, race or ethnic background may be deemed a "plus" in a particular applicant's file, yet it does not insulate the individual from comparison with all other candidates for the available seats.

The file of a particular black applicant may be examined for his potential contribution to diversity without the factor of race being decisive when compared, for example, with that of an applicant identified as an Italian-American if the latter is thought to exhibit qualities more likely to promote beneficial educational pluralism.

Such qualities could include exceptional personal talents, unique work or service experience, leadership potential, maturity, demonstrated compassion, a history of overcoming disadvantage, ability to communicate with the poor, or other qualifications deemed important.

In short, an admissions program operated in this way is flexible enough to consider all pertinent elements of diversity in light of the particular qualifications of each applicant and to place them on the same footing for consideration, although not necessarily according them the same weight. Indeed, the weight attributed to a particular quality may vary from year to year depending upon the "mix" both of the student body and the applicants for the incoming class.

This kind of program treats each applicant as an individual in the admissions process. The applicant who loses out on the last available seat to another candidate receiving a "plus" on the basis of ethnic background will not have been foreclosed from all consideration for that seat simply because he was not the right color or had the wrong surname.

It would mean only that his combined qualifications, which may have included similar nonobjective factors, did not outweigh those of the other applicant. His qualifications would have been weighed fairly and competitively and he would have no basis to complain of unequal treatment under the 14th Amendment.

It has been suggested that an admissions program which considers race only as one factor is simply a subtle and more sophisticated—but no less effective—means of according racial preference than the Davis program. A facial intent to discriminate, however, is evident in petitioner's preference program and not denied in this case.

No such facial infirmity exists in an admissions program where race or ethnic background is simply one element—to be weighed fairly against other elements—in the selection process.

In summary, it is evident that the Davis special admission program involves the use of an explicit racial classification never before countenanced by this Court. It tells applicants who are not Negro, Asian or "Chicano" that they are totally excluded from a specific percentage of the seats in an entering class.

No matter how strong their qualifications, quantitative and extracurricular, including their own potential for contribution to education diversity, they are never afforded the chance to compete with applicants from the preferred groups for the special admission seats. At the same time, the preferred applicants have the opportunity to compete for every seat in the class.

The fatal flaw in petitioner's preferential program is its disregard of individual rights as guaranteed by the 14th Amendment. Such rights are not absolute. But when a state's distribution of benefits or imposition of burdens hinges on the color of a person's skin or ancestry, that individual is entitled to a demonstration that the challenged classification is necessary to promote a substantial state interest.

Petitioner has failed to carry this burden. For this reason, that portion of the California court's judgment holding petitioner's special admissions program invalid under the 14th Amendment must be affirmed.

In enjoining petitioner from ever considering the race of any applicant, however, the courts below failed to recognize that the state has a substantial interest that legitimately may be served by a properly devised admissions program involving the competitive consideration of race and ethnic origin. For this reason, so much of the California court's judgment as enjoins petitioner from any consideration of the race of any applicant must be reversed.

With respect to respondent's entitlement to an injunction directing his admission to the medical school, petitioner has conceded that it could not carry its burden of proving that, but for the existence of its unlawful special admissions program, respondent still would not have been admitted. Hence, respondent is entitled to the injunction, and that portion of the judgment must be affirmed.

The *Bakke* decision stimulated much discussion and debate among professional educators. The American Council on Education issued a preliminary comment on the decision on June 30, 1978, which attempted to defend the procedures and standards of most existing admissions programs:

The six opinions handed down by the Supreme Court in the Bakke case require careful review before all of their implications can be known. Nonetheless, a first reading of the Court's decision indicates that race and ethnic background may be taken into account, along with other factors, in enrolling a diverse student body. We believe that the overwhelming number of admissions programs now in place meet the Constitutional standards as outlined by the Court.

This is a most important decision. In the last decade American colleges and universities have made considerable progress in broadening the composition of their student bodies. There is, of course, much more to be accomplished, and on behalf of the American Council on Education we reaffirm our commitment to overcome the effects of invidious discrimination and to provide educational opportunities for all.

Later, the American Council on Education and the Association of American Law Schools prepared a report on the *Bakke* decision for the guidance of law school admissions committees. Following are excerpts from that report.

The *Bakke* Decision: Implications for
High Education Admissions

The opinions in *Bakke* leave broad scope for discretion to be exercised by an institution in constructing an admission policy and by faculty or staff in implementing that policy. Indeed, the basic message of the Court may well have been that the question of preferential admission is one best committed to the judgment of educational and legislative policy makers.

· · ·

At the level of individual admission decisions, the Court has also demonstrated an inclination to authorize a broad range of discretion by school authorities. The Brennan group would permit use of race in the admission process so long as its use is not demeaning to any particular group and is designed to redress past discrimination against the target groups. Justice Powell's description of an acceptable race-conscious program is one in which extremely broad discretion is vested in the admission authorities. The Stevens group did not address at all the issue of the use of race in a flexible, discretionary program. Thus no Justice spoke against the use of race in a discretionary manner, and some members of the Stevens group might vote to uphold a broadly discretionary program even within the constraints of Title VI.

The courts have a long history of deferring to the judgments of an administrative officer so long as the office decision is within the range of discretion vested in his or her office. Lower courts have refused, for example, to review academic decisions on matters such as degree requirements and grades. In defining the permissible scope of an officer's discretion, however, it must be realized that certain types of decisions must be made within more narrow boundaries than other types.

The courts have, for some years now, consistently held that racial classifications and decisions based on race must be contained within relatively narrow bounds of discretion. Even outside the context of race, some writers have suggested that higher education admission decisions are sufficiently important that criteria of admission should be articulated and published to the most complete extent possible in an effort to confine administrative discretion. These considerations point out an inevitable tension between the concept of fairness, which implies uniformity in application of standards, and discretion, which implies informed judgment not bound by rigid standards. For Justice Powell and perhaps for other members of the Court, the scales tip toward the use of informed judgment rather than toward rigid standards in this instance.

The College Entrance Examination Board held six seminars on the *Bakke* decision in July and August of 1978, under the supervision of Charles M. Holloway, Director of Special Projects. It then circulated "Appendix C: Implications of the *Bakke* Decision for Undergraduate Admissions Policies and Practices," prepared by seven admissions officers of colleges and universities around the nation.

The report distinguished three different kinds of institutions: "open-door," selective but not competitive, and competitive colleges. The effect of the decision on the first group was held to be minimal, since normally all high school graduates or others eligible are admitted, and no other factors are taken into account. Selective institutions in which minorities were underrepresented could adopt or continue admissions policies taking into account race or ethnic background in defining admissibility. Because a racially neutral admissions policy would not ameliorate the problem of minority underrepresentation, the report argued that a "race-conscious" admission policy could involve the individual review of technically ineligible applicants to determine if the probability of success could be considered equal with those of minimally qualified applicants. If the minority-group applicant had an equal chance of success, in spite of low grades or college board scores, he or she could then be admitted over other students with higher scores on standard admissions criteria, but a lower probability of success. Competitive institutions could consider race as one of several factors that influence the admissions decision. Although the Court rejected the use of quotas, it did provide for race-conscious admissions decisions, provided applications from minorities and nonminorities are treated together, rather than being dealt with solely by race. The Court reaffirmed the traditional right of institutions to determine their educational policies, including their admissions processes. The report concluded that "it seems likely that institutions with well-conceived plans for increasing the diversity of their student populations, for example, a goal of a racial composition that resembles the racial composition of the geographical area generally served by the institution, will find support in the Court's decision on *Bakke*."

The panel concluded its report by recommending a series of specific measures that colleges could take to implement affirmative action programs.

1. Development within the admissions staff of special talents for minority recruitment; provision of the total resources to accomplish the college objectives in recruitment.
2. Identification and contact with promising students at an early age to increase the pool of potential college-bound students.
3. Effective contact with school counselors.
4. Cooperation with agencies and organizations that specialize in identifying minority students with college potential.

5. Development of adequate financial aid to attract and to sustain minority students.

6. Development of educational and student life programs which steer students toward success, thus creating personal enthusiasm which causes them to be effective recruiters themselves.*

The issues of affirmative action raised by the *Bakke* decision have been the subject of study by political scientists and public opinion researchers. In 1977 a Gallup Poll survey indicated that 83 percent of the American people believed that ability, as determined by examinations, rather than preferential treatment to correct past discrimination, should be the main consideration in selecting applicants for jobs or students for college; 10 percent disagreed. Early in 1979 a poll conducted by Louis Harris and Associates found that 71 percent of the whites surveyed agreed that "after years of discrimination, it is only fair to set up special programs to make sure that women and minorities are given every chance to have equal opportunities in employment and education"; 21 percent disagreed. By a 67 to 17 percent vote, a majority of whites favor such programs for blacks in industry, and by a 68 to 15 percent vote, they favor such programs for blacks in higher education.

Because of the wording of the two polls, they are not necessarily in contradiction. The first deals with the issue of preferential treatment, which most whites oppose, while the second is phrased in terms of programs to ensure equal opportunity, a concept that most people support.

A Gallup Poll conducted in January 1979 concluded that a large majority of college students thought that ability, as determined by examinations, rather than preferential treatment to correct past discrimination, should be the main consideration in selecting students for college admission. While whites in the sample opposed preferential treatment by a margin of 85 to 10 percent, nonwhites opposed it by a much smaller margin of 49 to 38 percent.

Without clear direction from the Court on exactly what was constitutional and what was unconstitutional, admissions officers muddled through, as the following story indicates.

---

*Reprinted with permission from *The Bakke Decision: Retrospect and Prospect*, copyright © 1978 by College Entrance Examination Board, New York.

Professional Schools Read Mixed Signs in Bakke Decision

Professional schools are now selecting their entering classes for next fall, and many administrators are finding that last year's Supreme Court decision in the Bakke case sent out decidedly mixed signals.

Interviews at more than a dozen campuses indicate that some schools see the decision as a mandate to alter programs that exclusively favored racial minorities. Others read the ruling as an endorsement of their affirmative action efforts. But few think they have heard the last word from the courts.

"The Bakke decision resolves nothing, absolutely nothing," said Harry H. Wellington, dean of Yale Law School. "I don't even know what the decision is. I think inevitably there will be further litigation."

After careful study, the New York University School of Law concluded that the decision placed its affirmative action program outside the law. The faculty voted last month to abolish a special committee that judged minority-group applicants separately, and to evaluate all prospective students.

Officials at N.Y.U. say the change will not undermine the school's commitment to affirmative action. But at N.Y.U., as elsewhere, minority students are fearful that the reaction to the high court ruling threatens civil rights gains of the last 15 years. "I think the Bakke case is going to put third-world people in a very precarious position," said Sharon Blackman, chairman of the Black Allied Law Students Association.

On the other hand, the Johns Hopkins Medical School in Baltimore has expanded its efforts to attract minority students since the decision came down last June 28. "I viewed the Bakke decision as an affirmation of what we had been doing," said Dr. John Yardley, associate dean for academic affairs.

Moreover, the impact of the decision is reaching beyond the admissions process. In order to avoid possible lawsuits, some schools are altering parts of their financial aid and counseling programs that favor minorities. Recently, the United States Court of Appeals for the Fourth Circuit cited the Bakke decision in striking down a rule at the University of North Carolina that guaranteed minority students two places on the student council and honor court.

The confusion has arisen because of the nature of the decision handed down by the Supreme Court in the case of Allan P. Bakke, a white who said he had suffered discrimination because the medical school at the University of California's Davis campus set aside 16 places in the freshman class for minority applicants.

Five Justices held that Mr. Bakke had to be admitted, because the school's quota amounted to racial discrimination. But, in another part of the ruling, five Justices said that race could be considered in admissions decisions in order to promote diversity.

Most schools' affirmative action programs began in the late 1960's, often under intense pressure from civil rights and minority activists. Many schools rushed to corral minority students, often without great regard for their abilities.

As a result, most professional schools have upgraded their admissions requirements, even though national figures show that this has contributed to a slight decrease in the first-year class in many professional schools. Some schools, as part of their post-Bakke analysis, have set minimum standards for all applicants.

Once such a standard is established, however, there are several ways an institution can choose among the applicants who meet it.

The most common method, and the one most immune to legal challenge, funnels all applicants through one admissions committee and establishes a broad goal, not a specific quota, for the number of minority students the school wants.

But, in order to get sizable minority enrollments, schools have to make race a major factor. At the University of Maryland's medical school, for instance, successful white applicants score an average of 10 out of 15 on a national admissions test, while blacks average about 7. Only one or two blacks would be admitted without special consideration, whereas approximately 20 are.

School officials generally believe that this sort of preference has been sanctioned by the Supreme Court, as long as the school does not rigidly set aside a certain number of places for nonwhites.

"On the whole, the effects of Bakke have been good and positive," said Donald L. Reidhaar, general counsel for the University of California. "Till the time of Bakke many people, including some of good will, had the gravest doubts about both the constitutionality and fairness of considering race at all in admissions procedures. I think that has largely subsided in the wake of Bakke."

Some schools have had to make major changes in their admissions systems, but these are mainly the ones that processed minority applicants separately and never subjected them to competition from whites. An example is the law school at the University of California's Los Angeles campus, which had set aside 25 percent of its seats for minority applicants.

Last month the faculty adopted a plan under which 60 percent of the seats will be allocated according to grades and test scores, and officials expect almost all those places to go to whites. The remaining 40 percent will be admitted on the basis of other factors, including personal essays, interviews, special talents and race. Whites who do not win a place purely on the basis of academic ability are free to compete for these other seats.

Supporters of the U.C.L.A. approach say it recognizes that some whites are also disadvantaged and deserve special consideration. But some members of minority groups feel that such programs threaten their hard-won gains.

In the end, the key conflict is over trust. White administrators say that many changes are "cosmetic" ones designed to satisfy technical and legal requirements, and that minority admissions will not suffer.

But many minority-group members doubt the good faith of institutions run by whites, and fear that the Bakke case will be used to cut minority enrollments.

"Ten years ago there was a real fear that if you didn't do certain things your campus would be occupied," said Stephen Carter, a black third-year law student at Yale. "It's not a real fear any more. There's not much pressure on those who are making decisions. The court was able to limit affirmative action because of the decline in social activism."

There is also a political aspect to the debate. Minority students at U.C.L.A. staged a hunger strike to protest the new rules, but they were mainly upset because the new rules cost them their voice in minority admissions. In the past, minority students interviewed minority applicants and had a large say in recommending which of them would be admitted. School officials contend that the students often used their leverage in the admissions process to win places for fellow activists.

Some minority students feel that the post-Bakke campus mood across the country has increased racial tensions. "Whites think blacks are there because of special programs, and that in effect we've denied one of their friends a seat," said Teresa Cropper, a third-year law student at American University.

Dr. James Comer, a black psychiatrist at Yale Law School, feels that the Bakke decision has increased pressures on minority students. "They feel they have to excel," he said. "There is a special consciousness of any errors they make."

Behind the debate over admission procedures lies another major problem: the continuing failure to expand the pool of qualified minority applicants.

The good minority students are getting better, mainly because they have benefitted from affirmative action at the undergraduate level and are able to attend better colleges. Almost without exception, however, professional schools say they still cannot find enough minority applicants who are able to do the required work. Last fall, the percentage of members of minorities entering law and medical schools actually dropped slightly.

Some minorities attribute the decline to the "chilling effect" they believe the Bakke decision has already had. Others are driven away by the high cost of professional education. But the main reason, some argue, is that society has failed to overcome the history of deprivation that weighs so heavily on many minority shoulders.

Some schools, including the University of Maryland, have instituted "pipeline" projects that select promising youngsters in high school and prepare them for the rigors of professional education. But there is still a long way to go.

"The job still has to be done at home and at the grade school level," said Dr. Morton Rappaport, associate dean of the Maryland medical school. "And that will take another generation."

You can understand the process of implementation of judicial decisions by finding out how the *Bakke* case has affected admissions policies at your own college or university.

1. Obtain from the admissions office the statistics for entering freshman classes for 1975–1976 and 1976–1977. Compare minority applications and minority admissions in those years with applications and admissions in 1977–1978 and 1978–1979.

2. Obtain from the admissions office the pre-*Bakke* affirmative action program, if any was in existence.

3. Obtain from the admissions office a general statement about post-*Bakke* affirmative action programs, if any now exist.

4. Using the guidelines developed by the College Entrance Examination Board panel as criteria, interview the admissions officers at your school to determine whether or not they have followed the recommendations of the panel.

5. If you attend a large university, you may wish to perform steps 1 through 4, using the law school or medical school instead of the undergraduate admissions office.

Note: This project might be carried out in cooperation with the campus newspaper or radio station. It might also be useful as a "team project" for several members of the class, with each student assigned a particular step to complete.

EXERCISE 9

The President, Congress, and Legislation

Presidents must attempt to lead Congress, for they need approval of their treaties and nominations by the Senate, and of their legislative proposals by both houses. But because they are often unsuccessful, political scientists have conducted many research studies to determine why presidents succeed or fail with their programs. In this exercise we will look at some techniques that are used to determine whether certain objective conditions (popularity, partisanship, national emergencies) are related to the passage of legislation or the use of the presidential veto.

A. Presidential Popularity and Passage of the Administration's Program

In this exercise you will learn how to make a simple correlation graph, useful in determining the probability that the existence of one condition is related to the existence of another.

Before constructing the graph, it is necessary that you understand the principles involved. Suppose we wanted to determine the relationships between growing apples and hiring apple pickers. We could go out to various farms, and find out how many apples were picked daily, and how many workers were being hired to pick them. Suppose we found the following results:

Farm A   1,000 apples   1 picker
Farm B   2,000 apples   2 pickers
Farm C   3,000 apples   3 pickers

We could say then that there was a perfect correlation between the number of apples picked and the number of pickers hired. We could also express the result by constructing a graph. The vertical axis would represent the number of pickers, and the horizontal axis the number of apples. See Figure 9.1. Note that each dot falls exactly on a line running at a 45° angle on the graph. This line indicates a perfect correlation between two situations.

Suppose, instead of the results expressed above, we found the following had occurred on the farms:

Farm A   1,000 apples   3 pickers
Farm B   2,000 apples   1 picker
Farm C   3,000 apples   1 picker

The graph would now look like Figure 9.2. Note that each dot now falls off the line. The farther away from the line, the less the correlation. The graph visualizes the data we obtained: there is no direct correlation between the number of apples picked and the number of pickers hired.

FIGURE 9.1

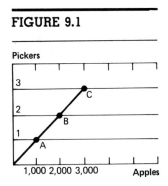

FIGURE 9.2

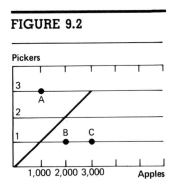

1. Review the data on presidential popularity scores in Table 7.2 of this Handbook. Calculate the average popularity for each president in each year since 1969, based on the data in the table.

2. Now examine the following data from *Congressional Quarterly Weekly Reports*, December 9, 1978, which indicate the percentage of bills supported by the president that Congress passed each year.

Support Score
1969 (A)   74.0
1970 (B)   77.0
1971 (C)   75.0

1972 (D)	66.0
1973 (E)	50.6
1974 (F)	59.6 (Nixon)
1974 (G)	58.2 (Ford)
1975 (H)	61.0
1976 (I)	53.8
1977 (J)	75.4
1978 (K)	78.3

3. You are now ready to plot a graph to see if there is any correlation between changes in presidential popularity and the rate at which Congress passes laws the president approves of. The graph has been started for you (Figure 9.3). It has a vertical axis, measuring presidential popularity, and a horizontal axis, measuring the approval rate of legislation. The letters A, B, and C represent the years 1969, 1970, and 1971. You should continue adding letters D through K, representing the years 1972 through 1978 (with two measurements for 1974, one for Nixon and one for Ford).

Do you see a close correlation between presidential popularity and "support scores" involving congressional support? Which letters are closer to the "correlation line," those representing earlier years, or those representing later years?

FIGURE 9.3

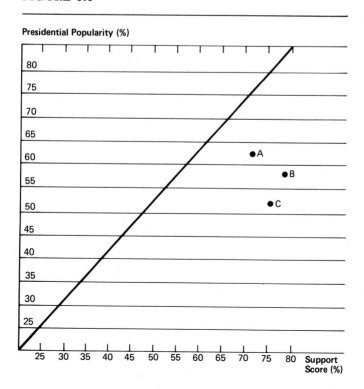

Presidential Popularity (%)

4. Now see if the pattern holds for the remainder of the Carter administration and for the Reagan administration.

    a. To find the presidential support scores for the years after 1978, consult annual volumes of *Congressional Quarterly Almanac.*

    b. To calculate public opinion support for the president consult the annual volume, *Gallup Opinion,* which contains the poll results on presidential approval polls for each year since 1978.

B. Use of the Presidential Veto

Increasingly the use of correlation techniques enables political scientists to formulate hypotheses about which factors in politics are related to other factors. Political scientists have, for example, tried to specify the conditions under which the presidential veto is likely to be used. One scholar, Jong R. Lee, traced the use of the veto from Washington through Nixon. Using sophisticated correlations, Lee concluded his study with the following statement:

Specifically, with other factors being equal, presidential propensity to veto increases:
    (1) when the president is a Democrat;
    (2) in an inverse proportion to the number of years he spent in Congress;
    (3) when Congress is controlled by the opposition party;
    (4) in direct proportion to the percentage of electoral votes he received in previous elections.

On the other hand, congressional propensity to override vetoes tends to increase systematically:
    (1) when Congress is controlled by the opposition party;
    (2) in direct proportion to the percentage of electoral votes for the president in previous elections;
    (3) when Congress convenes after the midterm election;
    (4) in direct proportion to the level of economic instability;
    (5) in an inverse proportion to the degree of military crisis.[*]

Other political scientists, while recognizing the validity of the correlations for most American history, have pointed out that the data may not fit the experiences of Eisenhower, Kennedy, Johnson, Nixon, Ford, and Carter. Listed below are public bills vetoed by several recent presidents. Examine the data and determine whether Lee's hypotheses fit them.

[*]Jong R. Lee, "Presidential Vetoes from Washington to Nixon," *The Journal of Politics,* Vol. 37, 1975, p. 546.

President	Public Bills Vetoed	Vetoes Overridden
Eisenhower	81	2
Kennedy	9	0
Johnson	13	0
Nixon	40	5
Ford	61	12
Carter (through Nov. 1978)	19	0

Which of Lee's hypotheses seem borne out by the data for modern presidents?

1. Did Johnson, Kennedy, and Carter, all Democrats, tend to veto more or less bills than Republicans Nixon, Ford, and Eisenhower?

2. Did Carter, with no congressional experience, veto more than Ford, who had a lengthy career in the House of Representatives?

3. Did Eisenhower, Nixon, and Ford, confronted with a Congress controlled by the opposition, veto more than Kennedy, Johnson, and Carter, Democratic presidents with Democratic Congresses?

4. Were more vetoes overridden when Congress was controlled by a party in opposition to the president?

5. How many bills did President Reagan veto in his first year in office? Does this seem to conform to factors 2, 3, and 4 mentioned in Professor Lee's study?

You can obtain information about bills vetoed by the president from *Congressional Quarterly Weekly Reports* and *Congressional Quarterly Almanac*. The text of veto messages is reprinted in *Weekly Compilation of Presidential Documents* and *The Public Papers of the Presidents*.

EXERCISE 10

The President, Congress, and Foreign Policy

Political scientists argue that there are distinct differences between the politics of foreign and domestic policy-making. You have seen in Chapter 20 of the textbook that the president acts differently and Congress responds to him differently when national security issues are at stake. In this exercise you can demonstrate to yourself that a president can often rely on public support and bipartisanship in Congress in times of crisis involving national-security issues.

A. Does the Public "Rally 'Round the Flag"?

Political scientists believe that in major crises the public tends to "rally 'round the flag," close ranks, and support the president as a symbol of national unity. After the Japanese attacked Pearl Harbor, for example, President Franklin Roosevelt's popularity actually rose 12 percent. The following graphs demonstrate other increases in popularity for Presidents Truman, Eisenhower, Kennedy, Ford, and Carter:

For Truman, Berlin and Korea

Percentage Approving

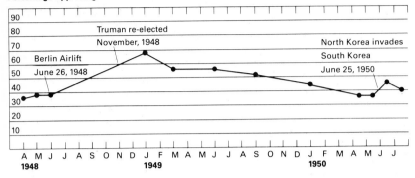

Note: Interview dates in June 1948 were June 19–24, 39%. In 1950, June 4–9, 37%; July 9–14, 46%.

Source: Surveys by the Gallup Organization, latest that of August 1950.

For Eisenhower, the Marines in Lebanon

Percentage Approving

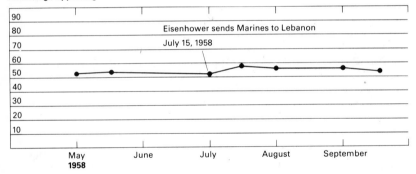

Note: Interview dates in July 1958 were July 10–15, 52%; July 30–August 4, 58%.

Source: Surveys by the Gallup Organization, latest that of September 1958.

For JFK, the Bay of Pigs and the Cuban Missile Crisis

Percentage Approving

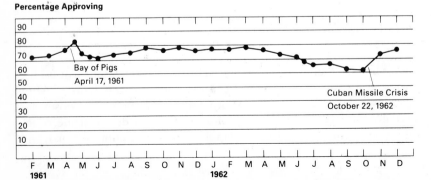

Note: Interview dates in April 1961 were April 6–11, 78%; April 4–May 3, 83%. Interview dates in October 1962 were October 19–24, 61%; November 16–21, 73%.

Source: Surveys by the Gallup Organization, latest that of December 1962.

And Ford, the Mayaguez

Percentage Approving

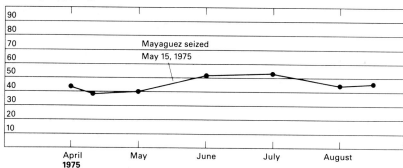

Note: Interview dates in May 1975 were May 2–5, 40%; May 30–June 2, 51%.

Source: Surveys by the Gallup Organization, latest that of August 1975.

For Carter, the Hostages in Iran

Percentage Approving

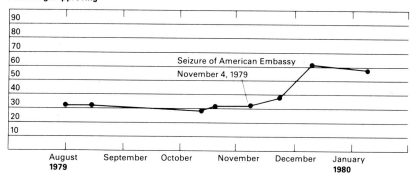

Note: Interview dates in November 1979 were November 2–5, 32%; November 16–19, 38%; December 1–5, 61%.

Source: Surveys by the Gallup Organization, latest that of January 1980.

But not all incidents provide this increase in support for the president, nor do all incidents provide a president with long-lasting support. International setbacks may cause a severe drop in presidential popularity. When Communist China intervened in the Korean War, Truman's popularity fell 3 percent. When Cambodia fell to the Communists, Ford's popularity fell 5 percent. And when the Vietnam peace talks were broken off in 1973, Nixon's popularity fell 8 percent. A president can expect increased popularity after an important international event, but he cannot expect the rallying effect to last long if his performance is seen by the public to be weak or indecisive.

1. Table 10.1 lists Gallup approval scores for President Carter.

2. From January through April 1978, the Senate debated, considered, amended, and finally consented to two treaties dealing with the Panama

TABLE 10.1 Gallup Approval Scores (in percentages)

	Approve	Disapprove	No opinion
1977			
Carter inaugurated			
February (early)	66	8	26
February (middle)	71	9	20
March (early)	70	9	21
March (middle)	75	9	16
March (late)	72	10	18
April (early)	67	14	19
Energy speech: "Moral equivalent of war"			
April (middle)	63	18	19
April–May	63	18	19
May (early)	66	19	15
May (middle)	64	19	17
June (early)	63	19	18
June (middle)	63	18	19
July (early)	62	22	16
July (late)	67	17	16
August (early)	60	23	17
U.S. and Panama agree to transfer canal			
August (middle)	66	26	18
September	54	29	17
Lance resignation accepted			
September–October	59	24	17
October (middle)	55	29	16
October (middle)	54	30	16
October (late)	51	31	18
November (early)	55	30	15
November (middle)	56	30	14
December	57	27	16
1978			
January (early)	55	27	18
January (late)	52	28	20
February (middle)	47	34	19
February (late)	50	33	17
March (early)	49	33	18
March (middle)	50	35	15
March–April	48	39	13
Production of neutron bomb deferred			
April	40	44	16

TABLE 10.1 Gallup Approval Scores (*cont.*)

	Approve	Disapprove	No opinion
1978			
Second Panama Canal treaty ratified			
April–May	41	42	17
May (early)	41	43	16
May (middle)	43	43	14
June (early)	44	41	15
June (middle)	42	42	16
July (early)	40	41	19
July (late)	39	44	17
August (early)	39	44	17
August (middle)	40	43	17
August (late)	43	41	16
September (early)	42	42	16
September (middle)	45	40	15
Camp David Peace Agreements concluded			
September (late)	48	34	18
October	49	36	15
November	50	34	16
December (early)	50	34	16
December (middle)	51	34	15
U.S. recognizes People's Republic of China			
1979			
January (early)	50	36	14
January (middle)	43	41	16
February (early)	42	42	16
February (late)	37	46	17
March (early)	39	48	13
Sadat and Begin sign peace treaty			
March (middle)	47	39	14
March (late)	42	44	14
April	40	46	14
May (early)	37	49	14
May (middle)	32	53	15
June (early)	29	56	15
Salt II Treaty signed			
June (late)	29	57	14
June–July	28	59	13
July	29	58	13
August (early)	32	53	15

TABLE 10.1 Gallup Approval Scores *(cont.)*

	Approve	Disapprove	No opinion
August (middle)	33	55	12
August (late)	32	54	14
September	30	55	15
September–October	33	54	13
October (early)	29	58	13
October (middle)	31	55	14
November (early)	32	55	13
American embassy in Teheran seized			
November (middle)	38	49	13
November–December	51	37	12
December (early)	61	30	9
December (middle)	54	35	11
U.S.S.R. invades Afghanistan			
1980			
January (early)	56	33	11
January (middle)	58	32	10
February (early)	55	36	9
February–March	52	38	10
March (early)	43	45	12
March (late)	39	51	10
April	39	50	11
Hostage rescue attempt fails			
May (early)	43	47	10
May (middle)	38	51	11
May–June	38	52	10
June (middle)	32	56	12
June (late)	31	58	11
July (middle)	33	55	12
July (late)	21	63	16
August	32	55	13
September	37	55	8
Election—Carter defeated by Reagan			
November	31	56	13
December	34	55	11

Canal. Using Gallup and Harris polls on presidential popularity and public attitudes toward these treaties, indicate whether or not the "rally 'round the flag" phenomenon occurred. How do you explain the drop in Carter's popularity at a time of a major foreign-policy victory for his administration?

3. In the fall of 1978 Carter announced the "Camp David" peace accords between Israel and Egypt, and in late winter of 1979 the treaty between these two nations was signed in Washington, D.C. Using Gallup and Harris polls on support for a Middle East settlement, indicate whether or not the "rally 'round the flag" phenomenon occurred.

4. Consider the changes in President Carter's popularity after the seizure of the American hostages by the militants in Iran. What happened to Carter's public support after the failure of the hostage rescue attempt? Was there a "rally 'round the flag" effect? If not, can you think of reasons to account for the poll results?

B. Presidential Support in Congress

In domestic affairs, as you know from your readings of textbook Chapters 10 and 11 on Congress and the Presidency, the president is often stymied by the legislature, with much of his program stalled, modified, or rejected. But in foreign affairs, at least in the legislative process, the president usually achieves much of what he asks for (the major exception being modifications in foreign aid and economic legislation).

Does the president achieve his goals because of party leadership and discipline? Or does he usually win foreign-policy votes because he can create a bipartisan coalition? To fully appreciate the lack of party discipline in American politics and the impact of bipartisanship on foreign policy, you should do the exercise below.

1. Obtain the roll-call votes (from either *The Congressional Record* or the *New York Times*) for the following votes:

   a. March 9, 1977, Paul Warnke confirmed as administration negotiator to SALT talks with the Soviet Union.

   b. March 15, 1977, Senate upholds administration position on ban of trade with Rhodesia.

   c. March 16, 1978, Senate consents to Panama Canal Neutrality Treaty.

   d. May 15, 1978, Senate rejects a resolution to block the administration plan to sell planes to Egypt, Israel, and Saudi Arabia.

2. In each vote the president won. Consider the partisan division. Could the president have won without Republican support? What do you suspect

would happen to a president who could not obtain a measure of cooperation with senators from the opposition party?

3. The AWACS Vote. On October 1, 1981, in the most important foreign-policy test of his new administration, President Reagan gave Congress formal notice of the $8.5 billion sale of AWACS and other arms to Saudi Arabia. It was the largest and most controversial arms sale in this country's history.

Congress had thirty days either to accept the terms of the sale or to "veto" the sale under provisions of the Arms Export Control Act. A majority of each house would have to pass a veto resolution for it to block the sale. On October 14, the House voted 301–111 against the sale. Attention turned to the Senate, which now held the entire decision in its vote.

For awhile the opponents of the sale seemed to have a solid majority. But in the final days before the issue was decided, the White House changed the grounds of the debate, from issues of foreign policy to those of presidential power and prestige. The White House argued that Senate rejection of the sale would critically damage President Reagan's credibility with foreign nations, and prevent him from conducting foreign policy effectively.

As the arms sale emerged as a question of presidential power, Republicans in the Senate began switching their votes. Of the fifty senators who had cosponsored a version of the veto resolution, eight first-term members—seven of them Republicans—reversed sides, citing the appeals from the president as the reason.

President Reagan personally lobbied numerous individual senators, using much of his political capital. He consented to a presidential letter of assurances, partially composed by several junior senators, that was sent to the Senate on the day of the vote. These assurances dealt with how the AWACS would be used by the Saudis—although the Saudi government did not give any assurances.

On October 28 President Reagan won his first major foreign-affairs victory, when the Senate, in a 48–52 vote, rejected the resolution to disapprove the AWACS sale. Obtain the results of the vote from *Congressional Quarterly* or *The Congressional Record*. Could Reagan have won this crucial vote had it been a straight party-line vote? Consider the problem of Republican defectors. Did Reagan need the votes of Democrats in order to win? Did he obtain majorities from both parties? Had the president not invoked issues of presidential prestige, do you think he still could have won?

C. Is There a National-Security Elite?

Political scientists and historians have argued the case for and against the existence of a "power elite" or "military-industrial complex" that runs American foreign policy. In the 1960s it was claimed that the Council on Foreign Relations was the elite group; in the 1970s it was supposed to have been the Trilateral Commission, and in the 1980s the Committee on the Present Danger. Gabriel Kolko investigated key positions in the national-security bureaucracy between 1944 and 1960, and found that 234 people held a total of 678 appointments, and that 84 of them had held 63.4 percent of all positions in those years. Richard Barnet, in a similar study of national-security managers holding positions between 1940 and 1967, found that these managers were, for the most part, outside of elective party politics, and indeed were nonpartisan in-and-outers, willing and able to serve any administration, whether Republican or Democrat. He also found these people concentrated in high-status professions and organizations: 18.7 percent came from very large and successful law firms; 17.4 percent came from major banking and investment houses; 13 percent came from the largest industrial corporations; 9.9 percent came from commercial firms; 7.3 percent came from elite universities or from the public service; and 31.6 percent came from career positions in the diplomatic or military officer corps.

1. You can analyze the origins and occupations of the national-security managers for any administration. You and your classmates can divide up the names of the managers listed in Table 10.2 for the Carter and Reagan administrations, or you can obtain more recent listings from this year's U.S. Government Organization Manual. Then, by consulting standard biographical sources (see below), you can find out what schools they attended, what careers they engaged in, and what government positions they held.

   Once again, it should be kept in mind, as the textbook has pointed out, that one cannot establish a direct relationship between people's origins or status and the policies they will pursue. But the study of origins, occupation, education, and status can stimulate thinking about the following questions: Is there enough occupational and professional diversity among national-security managers? Are any groups in society entitled to more representation than they now have? Why aren't blacks and women represented significantly? Since Barnet conducted his study, have academicians and government career officers occupied most of the important and sensitive positions? Are holders of doctorates in economics, political science, and natural sciences displacing the lawyers and bankers as national-security managers? Is there any evidence that most—or even a majority—of national-security positions are held by corporate, investment, or banking elites? By present or retired military officers?

2. The following listing, compiled by the *New York Times*, November 23, 1981, is of members of the Committee on the Present Danger who joined the Reagan administration. Do you find the argument that the Committee comprises a "power elite" whose members now dominate the national-security bureaucracy convincing? Or do you think it likely that some mem-

TABLE 10.2 National Security Managers from Carter to Reagan

Position	Carter Appointee	Reagan Appointee
Assistant to the President for National Security Affairs	Zbigniew Brzezinski	Richard V. Allen (1981) William Clark (1982–)
Deputy Assistant	David L. Aaron	James W. Nance
Office of Management and Budget		
Associate Director for National Security and International Affairs	Edward R. Jayne	William Schneider, Jr.
Central Intelligence Agency		
Director	Stansfield Turner	William Casey
Deputy Director	Frank C. Carlucci	Bobby Inman
Assistant to the Vice-President for National Security Affairs	Denis Clift	Nancy Dyke
Defense Department		
Defense Department Secretary	Harold Brown	Casper Weinberger
Defense Department Deputy Secretary	Charles Duncan	Frank Carlucci
Undersecretary, Policy		Fred Ikle
Army Secretary	Clifford Alexander	John Marsh
Navy Secretary	W. Graham Claytor	John Lehman
Air Force Secretary	John Stetson	Verne Orr
Undersecretary, Research and Engineering	William Perry	Richard Delauer
Chairman, Joint Chiefs of Staff	George S. Brown	David Jones
Army Chief of Staff	Bernard W. Rogers	Edward Meyer
Air Force Chief of Staff	David Jones	Lew Allen, Jr.
Chief of Naval Operations	James Holloway	Thomas Hayward
Marine Corps Commandant	Louis Wilson	Robert Barrow
Assistant Secretary of Defense for International Security Affairs	David McGiffert	Richard Peale
State Department		
Secretary of State	Cyrus Vance	Alexander Haig (1981–82) George Shultz (1982–)
Ambassadors at Large	Ellsworth Bunker Elliot Richardson Arthur Goldberg Gerard Smith	Phillip Habib
U.S. Ambassador to the U.N. (Cabinet-level position)	Andrew Young	Jeane Kirkpatrick
Deputy Secretary of State	Warren Christopher	Kenneth Dam
Undersecretary for Security Assistance	Lucy Benson	James L. Buckley

TABLE 10.2 National Security Managers from Carter to Reagan (cont.)

Position	Carter Appointee	Reagan Appointee
Undersecretary for Political Affairs	David Newsom	Walter Stoessel
Undersecretary for Economic Affairs	Richard N. Cooper	Myer Rashish
Director, Policy Planning Staff	W. Anthony Lake	Paul Wolfowitz
Assistant Secretary for East Asian and Pacific Affairs	Richard Holbrook	John Holdridge
Assistant Secretary for African Affairs	Richard Moose	Chester Crocker
Assistant Secretary for European Affairs	George S. Vest	Laurence Eagleburger
Assistant Secretary for Latin American Affairs	Terence Todman	Thomas Enders
Assistant Secretary for Near Eastern and South Asian Affairs	Harold Saunders	Nicholas Veliotes
Director of Intelligence and Research	William Bowdler	Ronald Spiers
Director, Bureau of Politico-Military Affairs	Leslie Gelb	Richard Burt
Director, Arms Control and Disarmament Agency	Paul Warnke	Eugene V. Rostow
Deputy Director	Spurgeon Keeny	

bers, initially appointed to the administration by Reagan, might have attempted to bring in other members who shared their overall policy views? In short, do you think there is a conspiracy, an elite group, or a "network" of friends that is responsible for the appointments?

Committee on the Present Danger Members in the Administration

Ronald Reagan
President of the United States

Kenneth L. Adelman
U.S. Deputy Representative to the United Nations

Richard V. Allen
Assistant to the President for National Security Affairs

Martin Anderson
Assistant to the President for Policy Development

James L. Buckley
Under Secretary of State for Security Assistance, Science and Technology

W. Glenn Campbell
Chairman, Intelligence Oversight Board, and member, President's Foreign Intelligence Advisory Board

William J. Casey
Director of Central Intelligence

John B. Connally
Member, President's Foreign Intelligence Advisory Board

Committee on the Present Danger Members in the Administration (cont.)

Joseph D. Douglass Jr.
Assistant Director, Arms Control and Disarmament Agency

John S. Foster Jr.
Member, President's Foreign Intelligence Advisory Board

Amorella M. Hoeber
Deputy Assistant Secretary of the Army for Research and Development

Fred Charles Iklé
Under Secretary of Defense for Policy

Max M. Kampelman
Chairman, U.S. Delegation to Conference on Security and Cooperation in Europe

Geoffrey Kemp
Staff, National Security Council

Jeane J. Kirkpatrick
U.S. Representative to the United Nations

John F. Lehman
Secretary of the Navy

Clare Booth Luce
Member, President's Foreign Intelligence Advisory Board

Paul H. Nitze
Chief Negotiator for Theater Nuclear Forces (TNT)

Edward F. Noble
Chairman, U.S. Synthetic Fuels Corp.

Michael Novak
U.S. Representative on the Human Rights Commission of the Economic and Social Council of the United Nations

Peter O'Donnell Jr.
Member, President's Foreign Intelligence Advisory Board

Richard N. Perle
Assistant Secretary of Defense for International Security Policy

Richard Pipes
Staff, National Security Council

Eugene V. Rostow
Director, Arms Control and Disarmament Agency

Paul Seabury
Member, President's Foreign Intelligence Advisory Board

George P. Shultz*
Chairman, President's Economic Policy Advisory Board

R. G. Stilwell
Deputy Under Secretary of Defense for Policy

Robert Strausz-Hupe
Ambassador to Turkey

Charles Tyroler 2d
Member, Intelligence Oversight Board

William R. Van Cleave
Chairman-Designate, General Advisory Committee, Arms Control and Disarmament Agency

Charls E. Walker
Member, President's Economic Policy Advisory Board

Seymour Weiss
Member, President's Foreign Intelligence Advisory Board

Edward Bennett Williams
Member, President's Foreign Intelligence Advisory Board

*Appointed Secretary of State, 1982

3. It is easy to obtain biographical information about government officials. You will find it useful to use these standard biographical reference works:
International Yearbook and Statesmen's Who's Who (London: *Burke's Peerage,* 1953–)
Who's Who in America (Chicago: Marquis, 1978)
Who's Who in Government, 3rd ed. (Chicago: Marquis, 1978)
Who's Who in American Law (Chicago: Marquis, 1978)
Directory of American Scholars, 6th ed. (New York: R. R. Bowker, 1974)
American Men and Women of Science (Social and Behavioral Sciences) 13th ed. (New York: R. R. Bowker, 1978)

4. The following individuals might interest you, because they represent a typical career path in national-security management. From the Carter administration: Zbigniew Brzezinski, Stansfield Turner, Cyrus Vance, Elliot Richardson, Paul Warnke. From the Reagan administration: Alexander Haig, John Lehman, Walter Stoessel, Laurence Eagleburger, Chester Crocker, Phillip Habib.

5. For less-typical career patterns, the following might interest you: Arthur Goldberg, Andrew Young, Jeane Kirkpatrick, William Clark, William Casey, James L. Buckley.

6. You can determine the continuity of national-security management from one administration to the next. This will enable you to draw some conclusions about whether or not a small circle of officials and former officials always dominate these positions. To complete this exercise, you will need volumes of the *United States Government Manual* covering the years 1969 through 1981. First, compare the names at the beginning of each administration from Nixon through Reagan. Is there much turnover? Is there continuity?

7. Perhaps there is partisan continuity. Consider only the Republican administrations in this period: Nixon, Ford, and Reagan. Are there any individuals now serving with Reagan who also held national-security positions between 1969 and 1977? or domestic positions then? Are most of the Reagan appointees holdovers from Carter or returnees from the Nixon and Ford years? If not, what conclusions can you draw as to the existence of a particular group of national-security managers?

2 3 4 5 6 7 8 9 0

106